PCs made easy

easy

STAGE 2

A PRACTICAL COURSE

Microsoft® Windows®
xp
edition

PCs made easy

easy

STAGE 2

A PRACTICAL COURSE

Microsoft® Windows®
xp
edition

PUBLISHED BY THE READER'S DIGEST ASSOCIATION LIMITED
LONDON   NEW YORK   SYDNEY   MONTREAL

PCS MADE EASY
MICROSOFT® WINDOWS® XP EDITION
A PRACTICAL COURSE – STAGE 2

Published by the Reader's Digest Association Limited, 2002

The Reader's Digest Association Limited
11 Westferry Circus, Canary Wharf, London E14 4HE
www.readersdigest.co.uk

We are committed to both the quality of our products and the service we provide to
our customers, so please feel free to contact us on 08705 113366, or via our Web site
at www.readersdigest.co.uk
If you have any comments about the content of our books, you can
contact us at gbeditorial@readersdigest.co.uk

®Reader's Digest, The Reader's Digest and the Pegasus logo are registered trademarks
of The Reader's Digest Association Inc, of Pleasantville, New York, USA

For Reader's Digest
Project Editor: Caroline Boucher
Art Editor: Julie Bennett

Reader's Digest General Books
Editorial Director: Cortina Butler
Art Director: Nick Clark
Series Editor: Christine Noble

PCs made easy – Microsoft® Windows® XP Edition was fully updated for
Reader's Digest by De Agostini UK Ltd from *PCs made easy,* a book series created
and produced for Reader's Digest by De Agostini from material originally published
as the Partwork *Computer Success Plus*
The new edition was adapted by Craft Plus Publishing Ltd

© 2002 De Agostini UK Ltd

Printing and binding: Printer Industria Gráfica S.A., Barcelona

ISBN 0 276 42753 X

CONTENTS

Windows®

If several people share a single computer, document storage can easily become disorganized. In the same way that things get moved around and mislaid in your house, so files can easily get lost on your computer's drives.

Whether this is because someone else has tried to be helpful and tidied up your folders or because you've accidentally saved a document in the wrong area, the result is the same: you can't find what you're looking for. If you use Windows XP's multiple user features (see pages 18–19), it will help to minimize the risk of other people reorganizing your files, but many families tend not to bother with passwords and user accounts. In this situation, being able to search your drive for lost files is invaluable.

The Windows Search command is a handy built-in file retriever that quickly searches through your computer's hard disk to locate missing files. It will work whether you know the file's entire name, a part of it or just a few words of text that the file contains. All you need to do is to give the Search command as much information about the file as you have and then leave it to do the rest.

● **First aid for the forgetful**
It's worth bearing in mind that Windows searches for exactly what you type in, so typing in 'programme' won't find a file called 'program'. This can also be a problem if you aren't sure exactly what the file was called. So what happens if you can't find the file name or the file itself doesn't contain any text that you can search for (such as an image created using Microsoft Paint, for example)?

Don't worry; you will still be able to track it down despite your forgetfulness. Windows' Search command will locate files that were altered between specific dates or a specified number of days previously. Providing you can recall roughly the last time you worked on it, you should have no trouble in retrieving the file.

Finding files

Modern computers have huge storage capacities and can hold thousands of files. If an individual file is 'lost' on your PC, Windows' Search command can soon locate it.

time you worked on it, you should have no trouble in retrieving the file.

Another problem that often occurs on crowded computers is that two or more files might have the same name, either because you have accidentally forgotten what you called the first one or because someone else has had the same idea. When this happens, Search will track down the name everywhere it occurs on your computer. But how do you know which of the files is the one you're looking for? Again, Search can help (see PC Tips box, left).

All in all, with the help of Search, there is no reason why any of your files should prove impossible to track down.

Searching by name

The simplest type of search is when you can remember a file's name but just can't remember where you put it.

1 Click on the Start button and select Search from the menu. A Search Results window appears, with several options listed on the left. For the most wide-ranging search, click on All files and folders.

2 For the simplest search, you need only type in the name of the file you want. We've used 'ding.wav' – this is a file that all Windows computers contain on their hard disks. Press the Search button to get Windows working on your search.

3 Windows shows the files it has found on the right of the Search Results window. You can see a file's name, together with other information about it, including its size and its location on your hard disk. The panel on the left now contains other options, allowing you to fine-tune your search, for example.

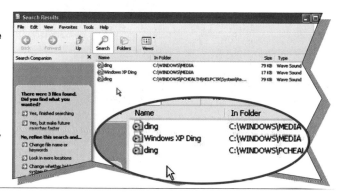

4 If you want to open the 'ding.wav' document, simply double-click on the name and Windows will open your file. In this case, it's a Windows sound file. Providing your PC has a sound card and speakers, you will be able to hear the sound file through the speakers.

Searching by date and file contents

Search will help you find files when you are unsure about what they are called.

WHAT IT MEANS

STRING

This describes a sequence of letters and numbers. Most of the time a string is simply a word, such as 'disposal'. You're not limited to searching for complete words, however. Search for the string 'dispos', and Windows will locate files which contain any of these words: disposal, indisposed, disposing, disposition and so on. The ability to search on a string is much more powerful than just being able to search on whole words.

1 Bring up the Search Results window, but this time select the Documents option on the left of the window. This type of search is faster than searching the All files and folders search (see Step 1, above).

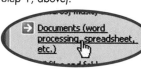

2 Search suggests using the date that the file was last modified to help find it. Click on one of the options and then click the Search button. In this example, Windows will find and list only those files that have been created or modified in the last week.

3 You can specify the search even more exactly if you click on the Use advanced search options link at the bottom of the window.

4 You can now search only for documents that contain a specific **string**. Type in a word or phrase that you know appears in the file you're looking for. We've entered the phrase 'offered the job' – this will help us locate the acceptance letter we created in the first Word exercise (see Stage 1, pages 34–35). Click on the Search button and Windows will then give you a list of all the files which contained the phrase.

Windows Task Panes

Look closely at many of the folders you open, and you'll see a set of links that can save you lots of time. Each one is designed to quickly accomplish everyday computing tasks.

With each new version of Windows, the programmers try to decrease the amount of work computer users have to do to get results. In Windows XP, one of the most useful new features is the Task Pane. This pane appears on the left of many windows and folders as a set of links grouped into boxes (see below right).

Although these links duplicate many of the tasks that you can achieve by using the window's menus or by opening other windows, they can save you lots of time. A little time spent exploring these Task Panes will more than pay for itself because you'll be more productive in the future.

● Folder differences
The contents of the Task Pane vary from one folder or window to another, depending on the tasks that most computer users would want to carry out in that particular folder or window. In computer jargon, the Task Pane is context sensitive – what you see listed in it is only what is relevant for the current folder.

For example, in the My Music folder, there's a link called Play all. This automatically starts the Windows Media Player program and plays every music file within this folder, one by one. Obviously, including this Play all link in all folders would be wasteful, as it's not appropriate unless there are music files in a folder.

● Extra features
Not all links in the Task Pane provide quick access to existing commands or features of Windows. As you explore the Task Pane, keep a look out for tasks that you might not even expect; some links may appear for tasks for which there's no other way of carrying out their action.

For example, in the My Pictures folder there's a View as slide show link. If you select this, Windows clearly displays all of the images contained within the folder in succession against a blank screen.

The panel of links on the left of each window can be a real time-saver, giving you one-click access to many tasks that would otherwise require you to select menu commands or even open new windows.

Exploring and using Task Panes

The Task Pane reflects the choices and options available within any folder, and the tasks you see listed depend on the folders you open and the items you select.

1 Click on the Start menu and select My Music. When the My Music folder appears, look at the Task Pane on the left of the window. At the top, a Music Tasks box contains two links. Click the Play all link.

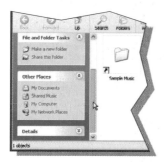

2 Windows Media Player starts with all the files in this folder and its sub-folders cued up one after the other (in this example, the two sample files are loaded). This one-click link is clearly much faster than opening Windows Media Player and loading the music files manually.

3 Go back to the My Music folder and look at the other tasks. Note that if the folder window isn't tall enough, Windows adds a scroll bar to let you browse through the full set of tasks.

4 Double-click on the Sample Music folder to see the files within. The Task Pane is fully context sensitive, showing actions and commands only when they are possible. For example, with no files selected within this folder, there's no option to delete a file.

5 However, as soon as you select a file, Windows changes the links in the File and Folder Tasks box. Now you can see several file-oriented commands, including Rename this file and Delete this file.

6 Now try selecting two files in the folder. Once again, Windows updates the links in the File and Folder Tasks box. Notice that while four of the previous links are still present, there's no equivalent of the Rename this file link. This is because you can only rename files one at a time.

7 One often-overlooked area of the Task Pane is the Details box, partly because it is tucked away at the bottom of the Task Pane, and partly because it usually looks blank. Select an item in the folder or window and then click on the small round button to the right of the Details heading.

8 The Details box now expands to show information about the object you selected, such as the date and time it was last modified.

PC TIPS

Other Places

Some of the most useful links are in the Other Places box. This lists several commonly used places on your PC, such as the My Documents folder and the My Computer window. The idea is that you can get to these locations from any other folder with a single click.

Customizing your Desktop

There's no reason why you should have to put up with your Windows Desktop being the same boring colours all the time. Here's how you can spice things up in a matter of minutes.

The first time you switch on your PC, the chances are you'll be greeted by the same green and blue colour scheme that every other Windows XP user sees. This standard look and feel helps to ensure that novice users aren't confused by wildly different colours schemes, but once you've become familiar with Windows, you may get bored with it. So what can you do to liven things up a bit?

The answer is customization. Almost all the colours and fonts of the elements that make up your Windows Desktop can be changed. It's easy to do and Windows even gives you a headstart for ideas by including some ready-made colour schemes.

● Keeping up appearances

We've already found out how to use Paint to create your own Windows background and apply it to your Desktop (see Stage 1, pages 70–71). Other customization changes can be applied in almost exactly the same way. Start by clicking the right mouse button over any part of your Desktop background and select Properties from the pop-up menu to make the Display Properties window appear. We're interested in the way things look, so click on the Appearance tab and you'll see a preview of your current colour scheme. Underneath are a set of buttons and drop-down lists that you can use to modify almost any of the objects shown in the preview.

Let's start by changing the scheme to one of the ready-made ones included with Windows. Click on the down arrow at the right end of the Color scheme box and select Silver from the list that appears. Notice how the preview changes to show you this colour scheme. Now click on the Apply button to change your Desktop to this scheme.

● Do it yourself

To make the biggest visual changes, you can switch to the Windows Classic style. This lets you alter every aspect, from the colour of the Title bars to the font used for menus. To do this, open the Display Properties window and select Windows Classic style in the Windows and buttons listbox, then click the Advanced button. A new dialog box (see opposite) lets you change individual Desktop elements.

For example, let's change the border colour of an active window to red. To do this, select Active Window Border from the Item drop-down list, click on the colour button and choose red from the palette that appears. The preview is updated immediately to reflect the change you've made and if you click on the Apply button, this change will be made to the whole Desktop.

You can make as many of these changes as you like. You can also change the size, colour and font of text items and the size of icons. You can even save your own customizations and add them to the Windows schemes.

By the time you have changed your background (see Stage 1, pages 70–71) and implemented the Desktop customization techniques shown here (below), your computer screen could look very different from the standard Windows XP set-up (top).

Customize your Windows

If you wanted, you could make your Windows Desktop match your curtains! That's probably going a bit too far, but you can still easily individualize the Desktop by following our simple steps.

1 The first time you switch on your PC, the Windows Desktop probably looks a lot like the illustration right. If you don't like this standard colour scheme, you can change it by right-clicking anywhere on the Desktop and selecting the Properties option from the menu that appears.

2 The Display Properties window appears. Click on the Appearance tab and you will see a preview of the currently selected colour scheme. In this case, it's called Default (blue) and is made up of blue Title bars with blue and red buttons, and a blue highlight for the button on the Message Box.

3 The Default setting is one of three supplied with Windows XP. Click on the Color Scheme listbox and you'll see a list of alternative schemes. Here we've chosen Silver and you can see what it's like in the preview window.

4 The preview gives you some idea of what a different colour scheme would look like, but the best way to test it out properly is to change the whole Desktop. Once you've chosen a ready-made scheme you like from the list, just click on the Apply button to see it in place.

5 To create your own colour scheme, first switch to Windows Classic style by selecting it from the Windows and buttons listbox. Then click on the Advanced button.

6 When the Advanced Appearance dialog box appears, click on the arrow at the right of the Item text box. Now you can see a list of all the parts of a scheme that you can customize. Select Active Title Bar and the colours for Color 1 and Color 2 change to that of the Title bar on an active window.

7 Now click the down arrow beside the two Color buttons and select two slightly different shades of red from the palette that appears. Notice how the preview of the scheme is updated to reflect the change you've made. Click on the OK button and then click the Apply button to implement this change for the whole Desktop.

8 Now you can experiment by customizing as many different elements as you like from the Item list. Why not try experimenting with the fonts? Remember that if you decide the changes you make are no improvement on the original, it's easy to restore the original scheme (see Back To Basics, above right).

Customizing the Taskbar and Start menu

As you make so much use of the Windows Taskbar and Start menu, it's a good idea to set them up to suit your own needs and preferences.

Located at the bottom of your screen, the Windows Taskbar is your main route to opening and managing programs. Windows is installed with a number of standard settings and, although these work perfectly well, as you use your computer more you will develop preferences about the way things should look and operate. Fortunately, Windows gives you plenty of flexibility to alter both the Taskbar and the Start menu.

● Taskbar options
The simplest change you might want to make is to the way the Taskbar is displayed. The default is that the Taskbar always appears on top of other items and so is always visible. Other default settings include large icons in the Start menu and the time displayed in the Notification area at the end of the Taskbar.

All these settings can be altered. For example, having the Taskbar on top means that some screen space is always taken up and not available for other programs to use. If you have a small screen or simply do not want to see the Taskbar all the time, you can easily hide it so that it appears only when you need it. The step-by-step exercise opposite (Changing the Taskbar options) shows how to change this and other Taskbar settings.

● Start menu options
Just as you can set up the Taskbar to suit your needs, so you can customize the Start menu to suit the particular way you work and make it easier to run the programs you use. While Windows XP remembers the six programs you have used most recently – listing them on the lower left of the Start menu – you can still add

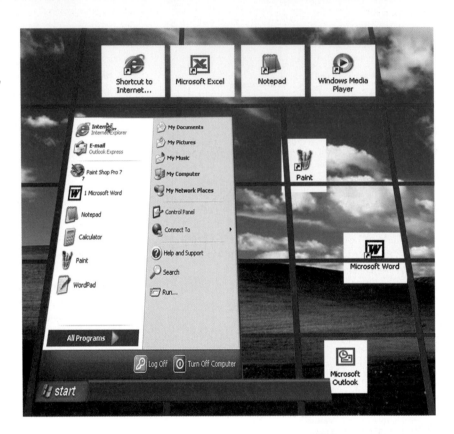

to the All Programs part of the Start menu to bring less frequently used programs to the fore. If, for example, you occasionally use Microsoft Paint, it can become rather tedious to have to click on Start, then All Programs, then Accessories every time you want to start the program. You could move Paint – or, of course, any other software you use a lot – to a more convenient place in the Start menu to make it quicker for you to reach. Try moving it from Accessories to appear under All Programs, saving one step, or move it to the top level of the Start menu, with your Internet programs, where it will be instantly accessible.

● Keep your options open
None of these changes needs to be permanent. You can easily change the Taskbar settings back to the default again or move programs around the Start menu if your needs change again in the future.

Changing the Taskbar options

The most useful Taskbar settings can all be altered in moments, making it easy to experiment and find out what suits you best.

1 Right-click on a blank area of the Taskbar. A menu pops up: select Properties from the list of commands.

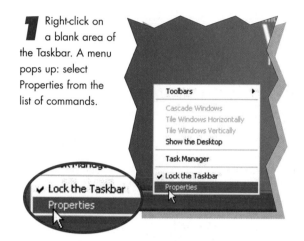

2 The Taskbar and Start Menu Properties window appears. On the first tab, Taskbar, there are two preview pictures that represent your Taskbar, together with a number of check boxes. When you select or deselect these check boxes, the preview picture displaying the Taskbar will change to show what effect your changes will have. The other tab, Start Menu, allows you to specify which of the programs stored on your computer appear in your computer's Start menu lists (see page 16).

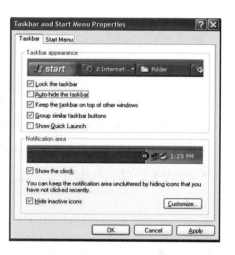

3 The first option is Lock the Taskbar. Click on the tickbox to deselect this option. You can see that the top preview picture changes to indicate that the Taskbar is now free to move (see PC Tips, below).

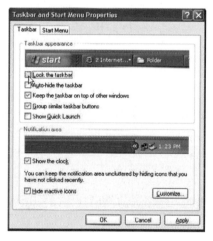

4 For many people the second option, Auto-hide the Taskbar, is the most useful. Tick this and click the Apply button and the Taskbar automatically shrinks down to a much thinner blue line, freeing up more space for programs. However, when you move the mouse pointer to the bottom of the screen it immediately pops up into view so that you can use it.

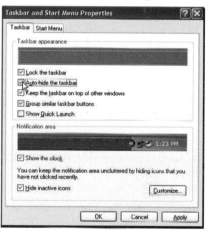

5 The Show Quick Launch option is also very useful. Tick this and a small toolbar of buttons is added just to the right of the Start button. Each button gives one-click access to a program without using the Start menu.

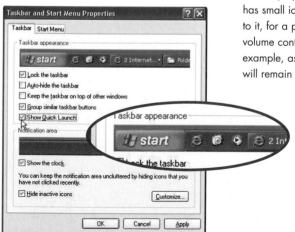

6 In the Notification area, there's a Show the clock check box. Its function is also pretty straightforward. You will probably have spotted the little digital clock display on the far right-hand side of the Taskbar and you can use this check box to turn it on or off. Don't worry if your time display also has small icons next to it, for a printer or volume control, for example, as these will remain in place.

PC TIPS

If you untick the Lock the Taskbar check box (see Step 3), you can move the Taskbar from the bottom of the screen to any of the other edges very easily. Click the left mouse button anywhere on the empty space on the Taskbar, hold it down and move the mouse up, left or right. You will see the Taskbar switch position. Release the button when it is in the position you want.

Moving programs around the Start menu

Whether or not you alter your Taskbar, you can change the way the Start menu works and which sub-menu contains what item. Here, we make Paint easier to reach by moving it from the Accessories menu to the All Programs menu.

1 There are several ways to alter the order of programs in the Start menu. One of the most powerful ways is to use Windows Explorer (see Stage 1, page 24–27). To do this, right-click on the Start button and select Explore All Users from the pop-up menu.

2 The Start Menu folder is shown open on the left, and the contents of this folder listed on the right. Don't worry about the lack of programs listed; many more appear when you click All Programs on the Start menu. Double-click on the Programs folder on the right.

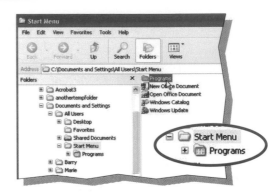

3 To move Paint from Accessories, we must look in that folder to locate the Paint program icon. Double-click on the Accessories folder in the list of items in the right-hand pane of the window. The list changes to show its contents. You should now see the Paint icon (don't worry if the other icons are slightly different to those shown here).

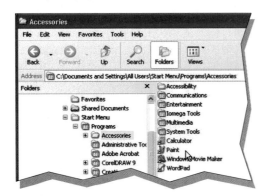

4 Click once to select the Paint icon, then choose Cut from the Edit menu. The Paint icon changes, becoming greyed (inset). This indicates that when you paste it to another location, it will disappear from this location. If you had selected Copy from the Edit menu, it would stay in this location when you pasted it elsewhere.

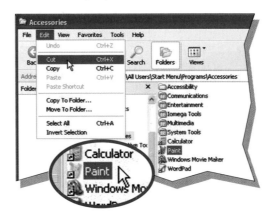

5 Double-click on the Programs folder on the left of the window to make it the current folder (notice how the folder opens).

6 Now click on the Edit menu and select the Paste option. You will see the Paint icon appear in the list of items inside the Programs folder (inset).

7 If you have finished moving programs around the Start menu, close the Windows Explorer window. Select Close from its File menu or click the top-right button on the Title bar.

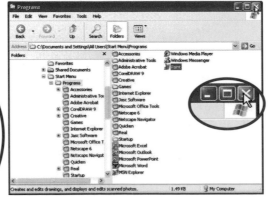

8 To check that everything has worked, press the Start button and click on the All Programs button. You will now see that the Paint program appears here. You no longer need to click through several levels of menu to get to the Accessories folder to start the program. We've shown how to move a simple Windows program, but you can do this with any program.

Faster access to your favourites

You can get even faster access to your favourite programs by moving them to the top level of the Start menu. Also, you can make them quicker to launch by renaming them.

1 Click on the Start button. Use the mouse to drag the Paint entry to the panel which includes the Internet and E-mail entries at the top left of the Start menu. A black bar shows the new position for the Paint program. Release the mouse button when it's in the right place.

2 The Paint program now appears at the top level of the Start menu. This technique for moving programs in the Start menu is a simpler alternative to that shown opposite, although it's a little less powerful. Unlike the program entries which appear in the bottom part of this panel, which change according to the programs you have used most recently, the Paint program will now always be close at hand.

3 Drag other entries for each of your favourite programs – you can also move entries from the All Programs listbox. As you do, the Start menu gets larger.

4 For the fastest access to these programs, you can add a keyboard shortcut. Start by right-clicking on one of the programs you have moved and selecting Rename from the pop-up menu (inset). Add a 1 and a space to the beginning of the program name, and then press [Enter].

S H O R T C U T S

Most common functions in Windows, and in the programs themselves, have keyboard shortcuts. These are very popular with advanced Windows users because it can be quicker to press a combination of keys rather than move the mouse to select options from the menus.

One of the more useful shortcuts is for the Start menu button. Just press [Ctrl] + [Esc] together and the Start menu pops up immediately. What's really helpful is that it will appear even if the Taskbar itself is hidden from view.

5 Do the same for the other programs you have moved, increasing the number in the prefix as you go.

6 Now your Start menu should look something like this, making your favourite programs easier to find. However, you can now also start these programs with a keyboard shortcut (see also Shortcuts, left). To load any of these programs, click on Start, then the appropriate number on your keyboard – 1, 2, 3 and so on. The program will load immediately – without any mousing at all!

Sharing your PC

With a little extra effort you can set up Windows to keep sensitive information from prying eyes and make sure your favourite settings aren't accidentally lost – perfect for family computing.

There's nothing more frustrating than sitting down at your PC to find that someone has reorganized the Desktop or changed the colour scheme to a lurid combination that makes it hard to concentrate on your documents. While it usually doesn't take you long to find your way around, or to reset your preferred colours, it's a problem you don't have to put up with. When Microsoft designed Windows XP, it decided to properly handle multiple users by providing user accounts.

● Business and pleasure

User accounts were originally created for use on office networks, where several workers have to share computer resources. In a business environment, access to commercially sensitive data must be carefully controlled by using passwords.

Similarly, with many parents now using computers to record family finances and children creating surprise greetings cards, user accounts on home PCs are just as useful. User accounts also help to avoid the problem of someone accidentally deleting another person's documents.

Not only can Windows keep each person's documents safe, but it also keeps a separate record of each person's own settings and preferences. If your child prefers garishly coloured windows, he or she can have them while Windows keeps your own choices safely tucked away ready for the next time you use the computer.

● Types of account

Windows XP uses two types of account: the Computer administrator account and the Limited account. The former should only be assigned to the

people who need access to the whole PC – typically one or both parents. They can then set up Limited accounts for each child.

Once these accounts are created, when Windows starts, the Welcome screen displays an icon for each person. This appears before the Desktop loads. Each person clicks the

icon for their own account and enters their password, and Windows loads their settings and preferences.

Limited accounts are perfect for children. They can create documents and alter settings just as normal, but when they try to access the folders of any other user, an 'Access is Denied' dialog box will appear.

PC TIPS

Logging on and off

When you set up user accounts, remember to use the Start menu's Log Off command when you are about to hand over the PC to another person. This command takes the computer back to the Welcome screen, ready for the next person to log on. If you forget, Windows assumes you are still using the computer and it will allow the next user to access and alter your settings and documents.

Setting up multiple users

Unless you set up user accounts for each person sharing your PC, everyone can see and alter everyone else's documents and settings. It takes only a few minutes to set up a more organized system which will prevent this happening.

1 The best approach to sharing a Windows PC is to get everyone to log on with their own user name and password. The first step is to open the Control Panel from the Start menu and double-click the User Accounts icon.

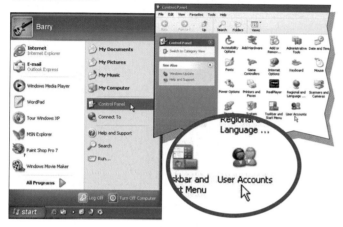

2 Initially, when no other user accounts have been set up, Windows XP assumes that the user is the Computer administrator. The administrator can alter all Windows settings and limit the types of settings that other users can alter, therefore it is best if the most computer-literate adult is the administrator. To set up a new user, click the Create a new account link to begin.

3 Use the next screen to type a name for the new account to appear on the Welcome screen and the Start menu. Then click Next.

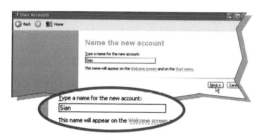

4 On the next screen you can assign this user one of two types of account, either Computer administrator or Limited. For children or those who might inadvertently harm other users' settings, select Limited. To give the user the same PC management powers as you, select Computer administrator, although it is probably best to have just one person in charge of these settings. Then click the Create Account button.

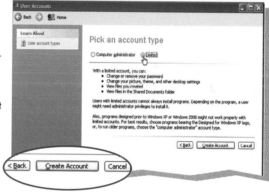

5 The new account is shown on the opening screen of the User Accounts window. To create a password (see PC Tips box) click the icon of the user you just created. A new window pops up – click the Create a password option and then type in and confirm the password.

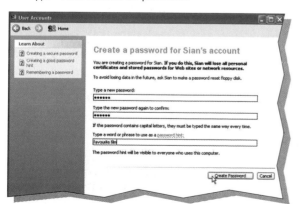

6 Windows suggests a picture to identify each account, but you can change this: first select the account and then click the Change the picture option. Windows XP comes with a number of icons. Select a different one and click the Change Picture button.

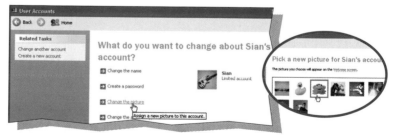

7 When you start Windows XP, a Welcome screen appears before the Windows Desktop and lists the icon and name for each user. Each person clicks their own icon to log in. Repeat the process to add other users to your PC.

Using the Recycle Bin

To avoid wasting disk space, you should delete files you don't need anymore. The Recycle Bin recycles disk space and gives you a safety net if you make a mistake.

K nowing when and how to delete files and folders is an important aspect of managing your hard disk. It is also extremely useful to understand what happens when you delete a file, just in case you remove something important by mistake.

You might be wondering why you should delete files at all, if there's a risk of losing important information. The answer is that by deleting files you can prevent your carefully organized structure of folders from becoming clogged up with redundant files. Old files make it hard to find the ones you still use and they occupy valuable hard disk space that you could keep free for new files.

● How to delete files

It's very easy to delete files. All you have to do is find the file you want to remove, select it and then press the [Delete] key. Windows will ask you if you're sure you want to do this. Click on the Yes button if you do, or the No button if you've changed your mind or clicked on the wrong file by mistake. The same technique works for deleting other Windows objects, such as folders and Desktop shortcuts. You can also delete items by dragging them to the Desktop's Recycle Bin; although, in this case, Windows doesn't ask you to confirm the deletion command so you should take extra care to make sure you are deleting the correct file.

● The safety net

You might have noticed that Windows doesn't actually ask you to confirm that you want to delete a file. It asks you to confirm that you want to send the file to the Recycle Bin.

The Recycle Bin is a special folder where Windows keeps all the files you delete. So when you delete a file, you're not really deleting it at all, just tidying it out of the way and into another folder. Windows does this as a precaution, so that you can get an important file back if you delete it by mistake. Just as with

a real wastebasket, you can reach in and retrieve something if you want to.

In time, your Recycle Bin will become full, and you will have to make a choice: you can increase the amount of hard disk space reserved for it or you can empty it. When you empty it, the files really will be gone for good. If you don't want to wait until the Recycle Bin is full before emptying it – for example, you might wish to ensure that private information has been permanently removed – here's an easy way how: just follow the steps below.

Working with the Recycle Bin

Sometimes you might accidentally delete the wrong document, while at other times you may need to make sure sensitive documents are destroyed immediately. Here's a step-by-step guide to using the Recycle Bin properly.

1 When you delete a file in Windows, it goes into a special folder called the Recycle Bin. You'll see its icon (right) on your Desktop. When the bin appears empty, it indicates that there are no deleted files in the Recycle Bin.

2 Let's create a dummy file in Word. We'll use this to illustrate how the Recycle Bin works. Open Word, type some text and save it as 'bintest.doc' in the My Documents folder. When you have done this, close Word.

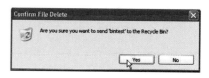

3 Open the My Documents folder. Find the dummy document you just created, click once on it to select it and then click on the Delete this file command in the File and Folder Tasks panel on the left of the window.

4 Windows always checks that you really want to delete the file. When it asks you to confirm your action, click on the Yes button.

5 Notice how the Recycle Bin icon alters to show that there's now rubbish in it: the icon appears to be stuffed full of wastepaper. This serves as a reminder that you have some unwanted files in the Recycle Bin.

6 Because the Recycle Bin is really just a special type of folder, we can open it to see what files it contains. Double-click on the icon and you'll see that it contains the 'bintest.doc' file you've just deleted.

DELETING PERMANENTLY

Although the command described in Step 9 makes it impossible to restore a file using the Recycle Bin's own commands, some utility programs are available that may be able to recover these deleted files. For total peace of mind with sensitive documents, you can buy utility programs that completely wipe the area of the hard disk used to store deleted files.

7 If you deleted this file by accident, you can get it back by clicking on the file and then clicking on Restore this item in the Recycle Bin Task Pane on the left (inset).

8 Look in the My Documents folder and you'll see that the file is back again. If you double-click on it, Word will open with the file ready for you to work on it. Now let's imagine that this file contains sensitive information – perhaps a letter to your bank manager – so you want to ensure that it is deleted permanently. First, delete the file as you did in Step 3.

9 To remove the file permanently (see Deleting permanently, left), double-click on the Recycle Bin, highlight the file and pick Delete from the File menu. To delete all files in the Recycle Bin, select Empty Recycle Bin from the Recycle Bin Task Pane.

Using Outlook Express

To send and receive email you need two things: access to the Internet and a program that can send and receive email. Internet access is easily arranged through an Internet service provider (see Stage 1, pages 136-139), and Windows includes a suitable email program, Outlook Express.

You can also buy and install alternative email programs. For example, you might find that your ISP supplies a CD-ROM that installs an additional email program. If so, you have a choice, and you can even use both email programs side by side. Most email programs work in a similar way to Outlook Express and many commands are almost identical.

● Starting with Outlook Express
Windows XP places Outlook Express near the top of the Start menu. If you have upgraded from a previous version of Windows, you may also have an Outlook Express icon on the Desktop. All you need to do to set it up is type in a few details about your Internet account (see Email account details box, opposite). Once it's set up properly, Outlook Express can communicate with your ISP's

POP3 and SMTP email services. You can then send and receive email with anyone on the Internet, as long as you know their email address (see Stage 1, pages 150-153). Your emails travel very quickly: a five-page letter can be sent in the blink of an eye and will usually reach the recipient within an hour – often quicker.

● Online or offline?
When you use Outlook Express, you can work online or offline. It's essential to go online to send and receive email, as the program must communicate with your ISP's email servers, but you don't have to be online while writing outgoing messages or reading incoming mail.

Working offline saves lots of money – it might take 15 minutes to write an email that only takes a second or so to send. Similarly, once incoming messages have been downloaded to your computer, it's worth disconnecting from the Internet while you read them. If you expect to receive a lot of emails – perhaps you want to sign up to a popular email mailing list (see Stage 1, page 155) – the ability to read the dozens or

Windows supplies several programs to get you started on the Internet, including Outlook Express – a powerful Internet email program.

WEB-EMAIL SYSTEMS

Most Internet users have an email program to send and receive email, but some prefer to use Web-based email. Companies such as www.hotmail.com have created free email systems to use through Web pages, rather than an email program. This lets you send and receive email from any PC connected to the Net – from an Internet café, for example. The disadvantage is that you must be online while writing and reading your email messages.

hundreds of incoming emails offline is very useful. It's the most important way that Outlook Express and other email programs differ from the many Web-based email services springing up (see Web-email systems, left).

● Plain and fancy text

When Internet email was devised, only letters, numbers and simple symbols could be used in an email transmission, and this is still the case. However, many people want to add the same types of formatting that they use in their word-processed documents. To work around this, Outlook Express lets you send messages in HTML form. Choose this option and you can add some basic formatting to your messages. Behind the scenes, Outlook Express converts the formatting to HTML codes that are included within the outgoing message.

In theory, when the recipient of your HTML email opens the message at the other end, the HTML codes are interpreted by their email program and the formatting you added is displayed. However, in practice, some email programs can't display HTML text, so the

recipient sees your message in plain text followed by lots of strange HTML symbols. Consider this when using formatting.

● Getting attached to email

Despite the technical restrictions on the types of data that can be sent via email, Outlook Express has useful features that can get around the problems. For example, you can attach any computer file to an email message. The file could be a CorelDRAW graphic, a scanned photograph, an Excel spreadsheet or a 25-page Word document. Other email programs will have similar features.

When you send such files through email with Outlook Express, they appear as attachments to the original message text indicated by a paper-clip symbol. Outlook Express encodes them so they get transmitted as a long sequence of letters, numbers and symbols. This all happens unseen by the users, because the email program of the recipient decodes the sequence and simply shows the files as attachments – exactly as they appeared when you sent them.

Email account details

You need to type some technical details into Outlook Express to tell it how to send and receive your email messages.

THE DETAILS YOU need – usually no more than half a dozen short but vital bits of text – will be supplied by your ISP. Depending on the ISP, this information might be added automatically for you. For example, some ISPs use setup CD-ROMs to guide you through the registration process. These usually take you online to register and then download all the necessary information in a few seconds. If so, you don't need to follow the steps

below – you can send and receive messages immediately (see overleaf).

However, a few ISPs require you to enter details manually. Thanks to the Internet Connection Wizard, this isn't difficult and only takes a minute or two, as shown below. You can also repeat the process to add extra accounts if you decide to sign up with additional email providers.

1 If you sign up with an ISP that requires a manual setup, you'll see a page of details for your account. Print or write down these details to use later with Outlook Express.

2 Once you've signed up, disconnect from the Internet and start Outlook Express. Use the Internet Connection Wizard to enter the details, screen by screen, starting with your name and then your email address.

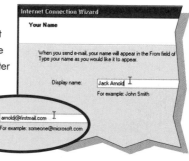

3 Now type in the POP3 and SMTP details, exactly as given to you by the ISP (see Step 1).

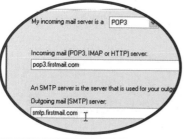

4 Type in your user name and password details. Leave the Remember password box ticked if you don't want to be prompted for your password every time you send or receive messages. Click the Finish button to close the Wizard. You're now ready to send and receive email with this account.

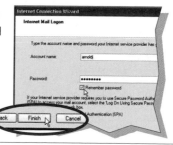

Composing and sending messages

You can work offline in Outlook Express to write your messages and then when you're happy with their content, just connect to the Internet to send them on their way.

1 Once your email account details are set up (see Email account details box, on page 23), click on the Outlook Express entry at the top of the Start menu. If a box pops up asking if you want to connect to your ISP immediately, click the Work Offline button.

2 When the main Outlook Express window appears, click on the Create Mail button. The New Message window appears: type the email address of the person you want to send the message to in the To: text box.

3 Type a title for the message in the Subject: text box. Notice that as you type the subject, the New Message text in the window's Title Bar is changed accordingly.

4 Now click in the main area of the message window. Notice that the text formatting toolbar becomes active. If you're sending a message to someone whose email program understands HTML, you can use these tools to format your message as you type.

5 When you've finished the message, click the window's Send button. This puts the message in the Outbox of Outlook Express. Click on the Outbox folder on the left and the area on the right will show the messages (in this case, just one) waiting to be sent across the Internet. A message box pops up to remind you that your message is only in your Outbox and has not yet been sent. Click OK.

6 It's important to remember that you must connect to the Internet to actually send your messages. Click on the Send/Recv button and then click the Connect button when Windows asks you if you want to dial up to your ISP.

7 Once you are connected to your ISP, Outlook Express starts to send your message. The bar chart and text area underneath show its progress. Don't be alarmed if you don't see the bar at all – short text messages take just a fraction of a second. Disconnect from the Internet when the progress window disappears.

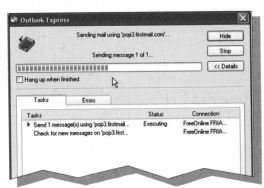

8 To confirm that your message has been successfully sent, you can check the Sent Items folder. Click on it to see the full list of messages that Outlook Express has sent.

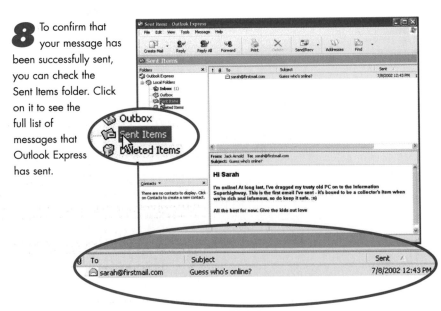

Receiving and organizing email

Check for mail and then organize it into tidy folders to avoid information overload.

1 Start Outlook Express and click on the Inbox. The first message shown is a welcome message from Microsoft. Click the Send/Recv button to connect to your ISP and check for and download new messages from your POP3 mailbox.

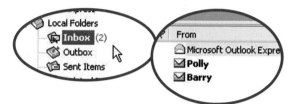

2 All new messages are downloaded and placed with those in your Inbox. The figure in brackets next to the Inbox shows the number of new messages downloaded. Click the Inbox folder and a list of your messages will appear in the top right panel. All new messages have a closed envelope icon to their left to indicate that you have not read them yet.

3 Click on the first unread message in the list and the message text will be displayed in the panel below. After a few seconds of displaying the message text, Outlook Express marks it as read, indicating this with an opened envelope icon. Click on each new message in turn to read it. When you have finished, all the messages will show an opened envelope icon.

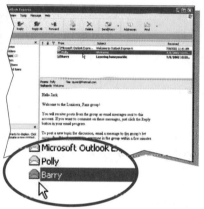

4 Over time, your Inbox will get crammed with messages, making it hard to keep track of different emails. You also run the risk of accidentally overlooking an important message among all the old messages. To counter this problem, create folders for long-term storage. Right-click on the Local Folders icon on the left and select New Folder from the pop-up menu.

5 Give the new folder a useful name and create others to help you organize your messages. You can make as many or as few folders as you like – if you share an email account, you can create a folder for each member of the family, for example.

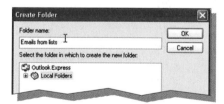

6 You can now drag messages from the Inbox into these new folders. This will help you to keep the Inbox contents manageable.

7 If you decide you no longer need a message, drag it to the Deleted Items folder. This works rather like the Windows Recycle Bin – the messages sit there until you clear them out, once and for all.

8 To clear out the deleted messages, right-click on the Deleted Items folder and select the Empty 'Deleted Items' Folder command. Be careful: once you do this, the messages are gone for good.

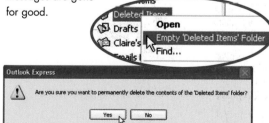

OPENING EMAIL ATTACHMENTS

Files sent to you as email attachments appear as paper-clips on the grey bar across the top of the message text. Click on the clip and a panel will pop up listing all the files attached. Click on one to open it. Note that Outlook Express gives you a warning about viruses (see also pages 146-149).

Outlook Express Address Book

You'll never be stuck without important details of colleagues, friends or family if you store their data in the easy-to-use Outlook Express Address Book.

Outlook Express is Windows' program for sending and receiving email messages (see pages 22–25). If you have Internet access, you can use Outlook Express to send email messages, photographs and/or computer files around the world within a few minutes. All you need to do is type the right email address into the To: box to send the message to the recipient of your choice.

However, typing email addresses into the To: box has its risks. Email addresses must be correct with all capitals and full points in the right places. You may accidentally mistype your friend's email address, possibly sending the message to somebody else or to a mailbox that doesn't exist, and in a few hours the message gets bounced back to you. By using the built-in Address Book in Outlook Express you can avoid these problems.

● How it works

To use the Address Book, you create a contact for each person you want to stay in touch with. Although the most important information to enter is each person's email address and you must type it absolutely correctly, without any spaces, you can also store their full name and various other details, too. This makes it a lot easier to find the right email address for each person – you only need to key in those strange email addresses, such as splodgy03@myisp.com, for example, once and the Address Book will record them.

Once their details are entered, whenever you want to send someone a message, you just

click on the small Address Book icon next to the To: box and then choose the right person from the names listed.

Although you select the person by name, Outlook Express inserts the correct email address automatically. As long as you spelled the address correctly when you entered the information the first time, every message you send will be addressed properly.

● Extra features

Although many people just use the Address Book for email addresses, it can store a lot of other data. For example, you can use it to keep a database of other contact information: telephone numbers, postal addresses, birthday and anniversary dates, and much more.

You don't have to use the Address Book to send email messages, but once you spend a little time typing in the details for your friends and contacts, you save yourself lots of effort every time you send a message – and there's much less risk of undelivered mail.

SAVING AN ADDRESS

You can enter an address directly into the Address Book or you can get Outlook to make the entry for you. Highlight an email in the Inbox, click on the Tools menu and select Add Sender to Address Book. A new entry is added to the Address Book and, as the information was copied from the received email, it will be correct. If you wish, you can edit the entry later to complete the details.

Introducing Address Book

To get the most out of Outlook Express, enter all your contact details into the Address Book. Here's how to do it.

1 Start Outlook Express by selecting it from the Start menu and then click the Addresses button. To start with, there are no contacts listed. Click the New button and select New Contact.

2 Use the Name tab of the Properties window to add the email details for your first contact. You do not need to fill in all the boxes, but it's worth adding first and last names to make contacts easy to find. Type the email address and check it is correct before clicking the Add button.

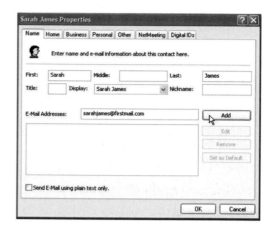

3 This email address is added to the panel in the centre of the window. You can add more addresses if appropriate – this is useful if you want to add both business and home email addresses for some people.

4 If you want to store extra information about the person, click on the other tabs and fill in the appropriate information. When you've finished, click OK.

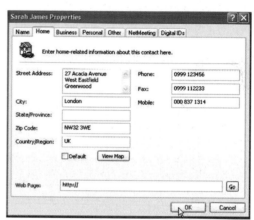

5 Repeat Steps 1 to 4 for each person you want to add to your Address Book. When you're finished, you can see them in alphabetical order in the Address Book window. Close the window to return to Outlook Express.

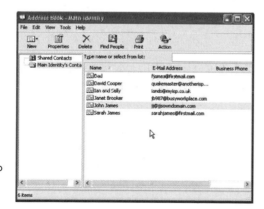

6 Start a new message In Outlook Express. Instead of typing an email address into the To: box, click the Address Book icon to its left (inset). In the Select Recipients window, click the person you want to send a message to in the list. Then click the To: button.

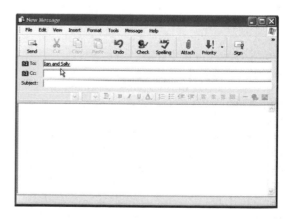

7 The name appears in the top Message recipients panel. You can add more addresses in the same way if you want to send the same message to several people at once. Click the OK button to return to your message window.

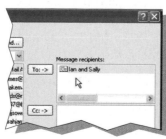

8 The To: box now contains the name of the person you selected. Note that this isn't the email address – Outlook Express displays the easy-to-recognize name you entered in the Address Book, and will replace it with the correct email address before sending the email message.

Software

CorelDRAW®

Check your spelling and grammar

You won't want to spoil the effect of an attractive document by making spelling mistakes and using poor grammar. So here's how to make everything you write word perfect.

How often have you seen an excellent piece of writing spoilt by a glaring spelling error or a jarring example of poor grammar? There's no excuse for your work to suffer from problems like this because Word includes features that can detect mistakes, draw your attention to them and suggest ways to correct them. In some cases, Word will even correct things automatically while you carry on typing.

● Word's wavy lines
You might have noticed that when you're creating a document in Word, red or green wavy lines appear automatically beneath some words and phrases as you type. A red wavy line beneath text is Word's way of telling you that it thinks the word is incorrectly spelt. A green wavy line under text is Word's way of telling you that it thinks you have made a grammatical error. There are two ways to get rid of these wavy lines: you can turn off Word's checking programs, or you can make the corrections and they'll disappear.

There are some corrections you won't need to make yourself. For example, try deliberately misspelling the word 'the' by typing the letters in the wrong order. Watch what happens when you press the spacebar to begin the next word. The correction is made automatically by a special Word feature called AutoCorrect. Word keeps a large list of common typing mistakes like this, which extends beyond spelling mistakes to include things like missing capital letters off days of the week. You can also use AutoCorrect to make Word type repetitive phrases for you.

Every document you create can be a masterpiece, thanks to the power of your computer's built-in spelling and grammar tools.

● Mind your language
As part of Word's installation, the program notes the language you type in. This is so that it can install the correct dictionary, grammar and thesaurus information to check your work. To make sure your system is set to the correct language, go to Tools in the Menu bar and select Language from the drop-down menu. Then choose the Set Language option and select the language you want to use.

Correcting your spelling

Word has a huge dictionary that it uses to check your spelling as you type. You can manually check individual words or let Word go through your document word by word, drawing your attention to any mistakes it finds.

1 As you type a document, Word highlights any spelling mistakes you make by underlining them with a red wavy line. In the first paragraph of this document, for example, the words 'dokument' and 'deliburate' both need to be corrected.

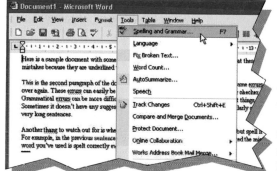

2 Let's use Word's dictionary to correct the first of these spelling mistakes. Click on the word 'dokument' with the right mouse button and a short list of options will appear. The word at the top of the list is the program's suggestion for the correct spelling. Simply click on it (in this case 'document') with the left mouse button to make the correction.

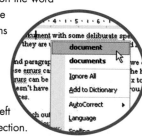

3 It would be tedious to have to correct the spelling of each individual word in a long document. Instead, we can get Word's spelling checker to work through the whole document. Position the text cursor at the start of the document and select Spelling and Grammar from the Tools menu.

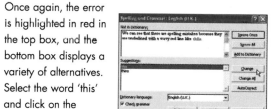

4 Notice how Word's powerful spelling checker immediately identifies the first mistake – in this example, the word 'deliburate'. The error is highlighted in red in the top box (labelled Not in Dictionary) and the program's suggested alternatives are shown in the Suggestion box. The top entry is highlighted. Click on the Change button to correct the spelling of the word to the highlighted option.

SHORT CUTS

Don't forget that you can use your function keys to start the spelling checker. All you have to do is press the [F7] key. This has the same effect as taking your mouse pointer to the Tools menu and clicking on Spelling and Grammar.

5 Word's spelling checker automatically searches for the next misspelt word – this time it's the word 'thiis'. Once again, the error is highlighted in red in the top box, and the bottom box displays a variety of alternatives. Select the word 'this' and click on the Change button.

6 The next mistake the spelling checker highlights is the word 'errurs'. Again, the mistake is shown in the top box and the suggested correction appears in the bottom one. This time, the same spelling mistake occurs several times. We can fix all of these in one action by clicking the Change All button.

7 The spelling checker moves on to the word 'thang'. Let's assume we often type 'thang' instead of 'thing' and we'd like Word to correct it automatically in future. Make sure the word 'thing' is highlighted in the bottom box and click on the AutoCorrect button.

8 Now we've reached the final mistake in our document: 'yewsed'. The suggested correction is 'yawed' but this is obviously wrong; it should be the word 'used'. To correct it, edit the word 'yewsed' in the top box and click the Change button to make the change in your document.

9 Now Word tells us that the spelling check is complete. Be careful, though, as the spelling checker cannot spot words spelt correctly, but used in the wrong place. Here, for example, we should have used 'write', not 'right'.

Making AutoCorrect work for you

Word can correct frequent typing and spelling mistakes automatically, leaving you free to concentrate on your writing. But you can also take advantage of the AutoCorrect feature to help minimize repetitive typing.

1 Word's AutoCorrect tool monitors what you type and automatically makes corrections if it spots one of the mistakes in its list. For example, let's see what happens when we make a mistake typing the word 'necessary' with only one 's'. Open a new document, type in 'necesary', but don't type a space afterwards. Word doesn't know you've finished typing a word until you press the spacebar.

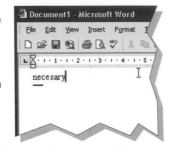

2 Next, type a space and watch what happens. Without prompting, AutoCorrect amends the spelling to 'necessary'. It also changes the first letter of the word to a capital 'N', as this letter appears to mark the start of a sentence. If this word wasn't in Word's AutoCorrect dictionary, a red line would appear under it, reminding you to check it.

3 You can view the list of common errors that AutoCorrect looks out for by selecting AutoCorrect Options in the Tools menu. In this example (right), we've highlighted the mistake that was corrected in Step 2. You can see here that you can also choose to automatically correct other typing mistakes, such as accidental use of the [Caps Lock] key.

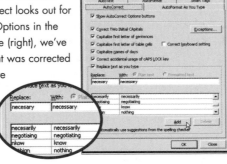

4 You can add to the list of errors that Word watches out for. Let's imagine that you frequently type 'bananna' instead of 'banana'. In the AutoCorrect dialog box, type 'bananna' in the Replace box, then type 'banana' in the With box and click on the Add button. From now on, Word will automatically correct this misspelling for you.

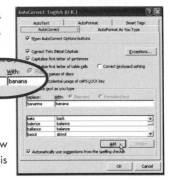

5 If you have a phrase that you use often, you can instruct AutoCorrect to automatically replace an abbreviated version of the phrase with the full one. For example, type 'mv' into the Replace box, then type 'The Merchant of Venice' in the With box and click the Add button. You have just told Word that every time you type 'mv', you want it to replace it with 'The Merchant of Venice'.

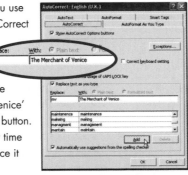

6 Now start a new document and type 'mv'. As soon as you insert a space after it (or a punctuation mark, such as a full stop or comma) AutoCorrect will replace it with 'The Merchant of Venice'. Remember to choose meaningful, but not common letter combinations, as otherwise AutoCorrect will change these instances of usage, too.

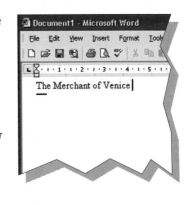

7 The AutoCorrect dialog box allows you to control other automatic changes in Word as you type. For example, if you type '1/2' (representing a half), Word will automatically replace it with a proper fraction character. Click on the AutoFormat As You Type tab to see the list of adjustments Word makes for you. You can turn these options on or off by clicking on the tick box next to each item.

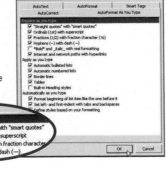

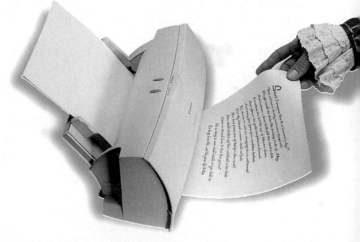

Increasing your word power

Once your spelling is flawless, you can use Word's other tools to make sure your letters and documents have maximum impact.

WORD CAN do more than just check your spelling. It has a grammar checking device to help ensure that your letters and documents are grammatically faultless and well structured, plus a thesaurus of alternative words to help expand your vocabulary and avoid repetition.

Word draws your attention to anything it considers is grammatically incorrect by underlining the text with a wavy green line. By default, the sort of grammatical errors the grammar checker picks up on include possessives and plurals, capitalization, punctuation and noun phrases.

● Check out those checks

To look at the various checks Word can do, highlight an unusual word in your text, go to the Tools menu, then click on the Spelling and Grammar option. This brings up a dialog box. Click on the Options button (inset, top) at the bottom of the box. The next Spelling & Grammar dialog box (left) shows the basic options for both spelling and grammar, but also gives you the opportunity to customize these options to suit your own purposes.

At this level you can tell Word which basic checks to carry out on your document by clicking on the white box by each option to add or remove a tick.

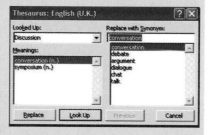

● Fussy about style

Word has two grammar options listed under Writing style (inset, bottom left). To change the checks you want Word to carry out, select which grammar writing style you want from the drop-down menu, then click on the Settings button. Simply click over the various check boxes in the scrolling list to turn particular checks on or off.

Clicking on the Settings tab when the Writing style is set to Grammar & Style brings up a more comprehensive list of checks that you can ask Word to carry out for you.

You will notice that the list also includes a selection of style options. These are not strict checks for grammatical errors, but are meant to help improve the readability of your work. You can get the grammar checker to warn you about clichés, sentence length, jargon and even unnecessary wordiness.

If you scroll down the list of Grammar and style options, you will find a whole host of checks that are especially useful in preparing long documents for study or work.

CHANGING SETTINGS

If you experiment with different grammar settings in Word then decide that you were happier with it before, don't panic! To restore the original settings, all you have to do is click the Reset All button in the Grammar Settings dialog box and you'll go back to square one.

Thesaurus facility

To find another word for one you've already used a lot, Word's built-in thesaurus will help. Click the cursor on the word you want to look up and press the [Shift]+[F7] keys. The Thesaurus dialog box will show your word in the top left box and, below it, a selection of possible meanings. A list of synonyms or related words is given for each meaning, with the currently selected word shown above it. Use the two lists to choose the word you want and click on the Replace button to change the word in your document.

Introducing Word's Task Panes

The options listed in the default Task Pane appear trivial, but in addition to basic commands, Word's Task Panes make powerful features easy to use.

The Task Pane appears in each of Microsoft's Office XP suite of programs – including Word 2002 and Excel 2002. It's a narrow column of options and commands on the far right of the screen. You may already be using the commands on the default Task Pane, called New Documents, or you may have thought it too basic and turned it off (see Task Pane option below). However, there are several Task Panes and some give you access to powerful features of Word. It's well worth taking a little time to explore them and see how they can save you time and effort.

● **Task Pane principles**
The idea behind the Task Pane is that it speeds up your work. By bringing common and useful tasks to the fore, it allows you to issue commands with fewer clicks. However, that's only part of the appeal – some of Word's more advanced features are a lot easier to use through the Task Pane. For example, the Task Pane for Mail Merge leads you through the process of creating mailshots (we'll cover this useful process later in the course).

Other Task Panes present information and choices that would be awkward to access via menus or dialog boxes. For instance, the Reveal Formatting Task Pane lets you see at a glance all aspects of the formatting for any part of a document. This can help you spot and fix any inconsistencies that might otherwise spoil the look of the printed document. A key benefit of this Task Pane is that there's no need to remember which

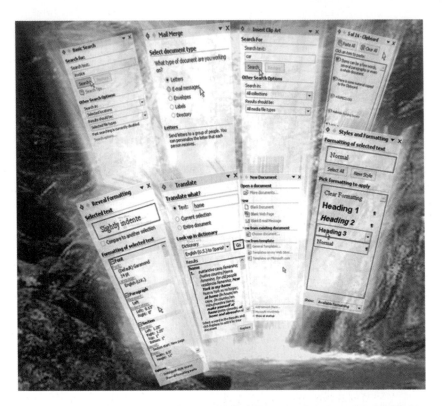

There are eight Task Panes to cover the most frequently used commands in Word.

command brings up the appropriate dialog box for altering the formatting. You can use the links in the Task Pane to jump directly to the correct dialog box.

● **Experiment and familiarize**
There are eight Task Panes in all – including one for Word's basic language translation feature – and each one can help you get quicker results for a range of different tasks. So, don't be tempted to turn off the Task Pane too quickly – you're bound to find some useful shortcuts and functions.

TASK PANE OPTION

If you prefer working with Word's normal menu and toolbar commands, you can obtain the biggest document area possible by telling Word not to display the Task Pane every time it starts. Untick the Show at startup box at the bottom of the Task Pane.

PC TIPS

Office bonus
If you use the Office XP suite of programs, you will find that the Clipboard Task Pane is especially useful. At its most basic, Word's Clipboard builds on the basic Clipboard feature of Windows (see Stage 1, pages 16–17), storing up to 24 items at a time. However, as an added bonus, the Clipboard Task Pane also makes it a cinch to copy and paste items between the various different Office programs.

Choosing and using Task Panes

There are eight Task Panes to choose from in Word, covering simple document commands to more advanced formatting and style options. Each one helps you create and format documents efficiently.

1 The Task Pane appears as a column on the right side of the Word window. If it isn't visible, select Task Pane from the View menu (inset) to make it appear.

2 By default, the New Document Task Pane appears. This contains basic commands aimed at making it faster to create new documents or open existing ones. For example, at the top of the Task Pane there's a list of the documents you have been working on recently; one click loads the document.

3 Select the Styles and Formatting Task Pane from the drop-down menu that appears when you click on the downward-pointing arrow next to the Task Pane title.

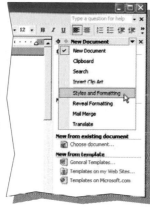

4 This pane shows each of the styles directly, and applying any style is a simple case of selecting the relevant text and clicking on the formatting that you want from the Task Pane. You can experiment quickly and easily. (For more on styles see pages 46–49.)

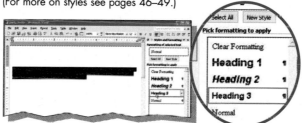

5 Word comes with some basic translation features (see PC Tips, right). Select the Translate Task Pane and type a word into the text box under the Translate what? heading. Then select one of the Dictionary settings. Click the Go button. If this is the first time you've tried translation, Word may ask if want to install this feature. Click the Yes button.

6 Within a few moments a basic translation appears in the Task Pane (inset), with some extra examples based around the word you typed in to make sure you can choose the right one for the context.

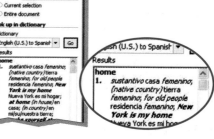

7 Now choose the Reveal Formatting Task Pane. Create a document that contains several different types of formatting and then move the text cursor around the document. Notice that the Task Pane tells you everything about the formatting for the text.

8 If you spot any aspect of formatting that you want to change, you can go directly to the appropriate formatting dialog box by simply clicking on the blue underlined link in the Task Pane. (See pages 46–49 for more details on styling and formatting text.) You can even set the formatting before you start typing your document by clicking on the default items in the Reveal Formatting Task Pane (see Step 7).

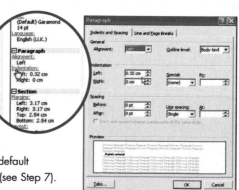

Creating tables

Many of the documents you are creating work best in table form, for example, a birthday present list or a packing checklist for going on holiday. Here we show you the easy way to set up tables in a word-processing program.

Item	Reference No.	Number Required	Price per unit	Total Price
Chisel	GF495345	1	£ 7.99	£ 7.99
Shelf	SI495959	3	£ 12.95	£ 38.85
Ladder	OI450939	1	£ 29.99	£ 29.99
Masonry Nails	IF488458	12	£ 4.99	£ 59.88
Hammer	EI403821	1	£ 6.99	£ 6.99
Paint	PV94959	6	£ 9.99	£ 59.94
				£ 203.64

Date	Expenses		
12/9/00	Train Fare	£ 34.9	
14/9/00	Meals	£ 12.9	
22/9/00	Petrol	£ 20	
28/9/00	Petrol & Meals		
1/10/00	Train Fare & Taxi		

Airport	Date	Time
Gatwick	6 July 2000	063
	2000	21
	000	04

Creating lists in a Word document is quite a common requirement, whether it's the shopping list, a 'to-do' list or a birthday card list. For the most basic of lists (usually those with only one column), most people simply use the [Tab] key (see Stage 1, page 34). This indents the items in the list, so that it stands out from the main body of the text. However, for more complex lists, you will need to create a table so the content is legible.

In our step-by-step examples on pages 38–39, we show you how to compile a list of birthday presents, using the person's name, date of birth and what present they would like. This list will illustrate most of the common steps involved in making and adjusting tables, in particular adding new rows and information. With Word tables, you can easily add something you've forgotten, in this case an extra child's or adult's birthday.

● **Simplified spreadsheet**

A table works much like a simplified spreadsheet. It looks similar, too, with rows and columns of cells into which you can type your information. A Word table is not as restrictive as a spreadsheet, in that the word processor doesn't mind whether you type in numbers or letters. However, it doesn't allow you to make complex maths calculations on the contents of the table in the way that Excel does. In Word, a table is more likely to be used to make your document look more professional and easy to read, rather than for calculations. As you will see from the list of birthday presents, it is easier to read and alter than a hand-written note stuck to the fridge.

● **Great for lists**

Although we won't explore it in detail now, Word can also do some simple mathematics with any numerical data you enter in the cells, much like a mini-spreadsheet. It is because of this versatility, combined with the ease of changing the look and format of boxes, that many people find Word's tables useful for list-based jobs. You can see from the examples opposite how anything from an order form to a business invoice can be created as a list, quickly and professionally, and still form part of a larger document or letter.

WHAT IT MEANS

CELLS
Each box in a table is called a cell. This is also the word used to describe the boxes in spreadsheets. In Word tables, each cell can be altered in size, either individually or as part of a whole column or row. To type text, select a cell by clicking on it with the mouse or by moving the text insertion point around the table with the cursor arrow keys.

Making use of tables

Tables can be used to tidy up all sorts of documents. As Word lets you include them in letters or other documents, you can use tables to make any kind of list-based information stand out.

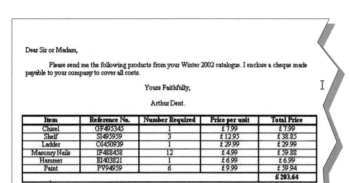

Order forms

Whenever you shop by mail order, it's important to make your orders clear. By compiling a five-column list containing the item required, the reference number, the number of items required, the price per item and the total price, you should remove any chance of misunderstanding. This example uses a simple grid to make the table easy to read, both across and down.

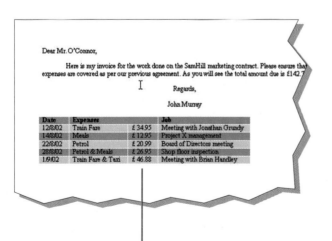

Easy-to-read invoices

For anyone running a small business or providing any sort of service, Word makes it simple to set up easy-to-read invoices. This itemized expenses bill consists of a table with four columns. Note that the third column does not need a heading. This example uses shaded backgrounds to make it easy to read across the rows.

Travel timetables

Itemized timetables and travel arrangements are always easier to read in table form. This example uses seven columns. The headings are bold to emphasize the key information and make the table simpler to follow.

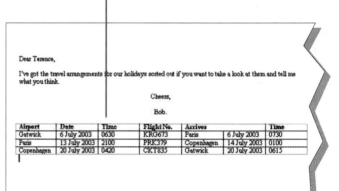

Using colours to lift lists

This reading list for a child demonstrates how using different colours makes it easier to read across the table. It also shows the benefit of using bold text in one column to emphasize the most important information – in this case, to pick out the title of the book.

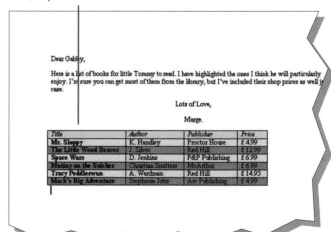

Creating a simple table

For this example, we'll create a short table to store information about the birthday presents given to each of seven children.

1 Position the text cursor in the document where you want the table to be. Choose Insert then Table from the drop-down Table menu.

2 The table needs three columns and eight rows, so type '3' in the Number of columns box and type '8' in the Number of rows box.

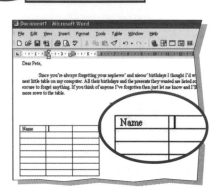

3 We need to give the width of each column to ensure it doesn't run off the edge of an A4 sheet of paper when printed. In the Fixed column width box, type '2'. This creates a column 2cm wide. (If the width you choose turns out to be too narrow, you can alter the column width later.) Then click OK.

4 A blank table with three columns and eight rows will appear on the screen. Click on the top left cell and start typing in your information. You can move around the table cells with your mouse or, if you prefer, you can use the cursor keys or even the [Tab] key.

5 You can follow our example or make up your own entries. Notice how it doesn't matter if the entry is too long to fit into the width of a cell (as with 'Date of Birth' in the second cell in the top row). Word automatically puts in a second line to make room. This applies to whichever cell is affected.

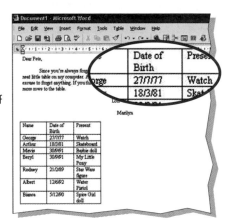

6 The normal text-formatting commands also work inside tables. To make all the column headings bold, place your mouse pointer to the left of the top Name cell, so that it appears to point towards it at an angle (inset). Now click once and the entire top row becomes highlighted (right). If you click on the Bold button in the toolbar, all the column headers will appear in bold (inset, right).

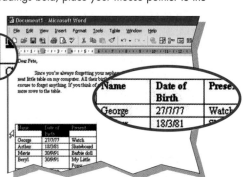

7 You can also edit individual entries. Move the pointer towards the left edge of the 'Star Wars figure' text; it changes to a small black arrow pointing to the right. Click once and this cell will be highlighted. Click on the Italic button in the toolbar to italicize this text.

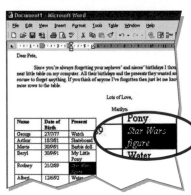

8 You can align text in columns in the same way as you would normal text. Move your mouse pointer to just above the top of the middle column. The cursor will change into a downward pointing arrow (inset, left). Click once and the whole column will be highlighted. Now choose the Center button in the toolbar and the text will centre in the cells (inset, right). Feel free to experiment with other columns to see how the Align Right and Justify buttons affect the look of the text in the cells. Make sure you save the table for the exercise opposite, which explores more table features.

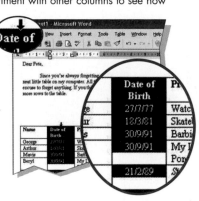

PC TIPS

If you want to draw a table quickly, there is an alternative to using the Table menu. Click the Insert Table icon on the toolbar (right), and you will see a grid that lets you select the size and format of a table (below). Drag your mouse diagonally from the top left square to select the number of rows and columns you want. Release the mouse button. With this method, Word will automatically specify the width of columns, but you can change them once the table has been drawn.

Fine tuning the look of your table

Here's how to modify the size of existing cells and add extra information to the table we created in the previous exercise.

1 In the example we created on the opposite page, you saw how Word increases the depth of a cell to accommodate long words or a group of words that don't fit into the width of a single cell. This can make the table look uneven and hard to read, but the width of the cells can be altered to tidy things up.

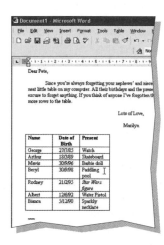

2 To alter the size of a cell, move the mouse pointer over the right border of the cell containing the long word or group of words. Your cursor will then turn into two arrowed, vertical lines (inset). Click and hold the left mouse button. Now move your mouse to the right and a dotted line will appear to show you the new column width (right). When it is long enough for all the words to fit on a single line, release the mouse button.

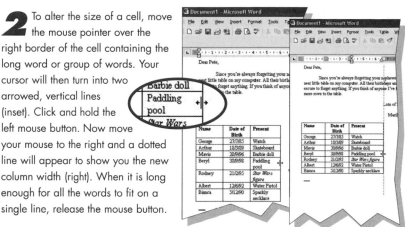

3 Sometimes, you might wish to increase the width of a single cell, perhaps to ensure that the title of a column stays on one line. Highlight the cell as before by clicking close to its left edge. Now move the cursor on to the right column divider until the cursor changes, then increase the width of the cell as you did in Step 2 of this exercise.

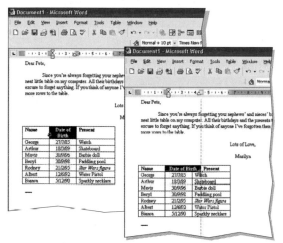

4 A common problem is needing to add extra rows of information after the table has been created. This is easy, as you can add the row at any point in the table. Highlight the row above which you want the new row to appear. Now go to the Table menu and select Insert, then choose Rows Above from the drop-down menu.

SHORT CUTS

If you want to apply the same formatting to all the text in a table, click once within the table, then select it all by holding down the [Alt] key and pressing [5] on the numeric keypad (usually on the right of your keyboard). Before doing this, make sure that NumLock is switched off (see Stage 1, page 95).

5 A blank row of highlighted cells appears. Now you can add details of another name, birthday and present, as before. You can see with the final table (below right) how these few tricks can change the look and contents of a table.

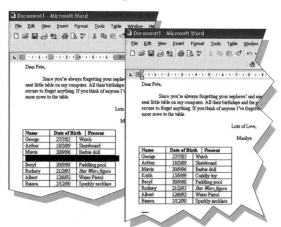

NUMBER COLUMNS

Text alignment is a useful tool for many different purposes, not just for making the table look neat. Often, your table will include a price column and a total price. It's useful if this can be checked or added to easily. If you align the numbers to the right when they are entered, the prices will be arranged into pounds and pence columns aligned to the decimal point.

Price per unit	Total Price
£7.99	£7.99
£12.95	£38.85
£29.99	£29.99
£4.99	£59.88
£6.99	£6.99
£9.99	£59.94
	£203.64

Perfect paragraphs

Formatting can be applied to a whole paragraph in a Word document. You can also control margins, indents and spacing – and it is possible to do it all from one place, making sure each document has the best layout for its purpose.

W e've already seen how you can format text in a Word document (see Stage 1, pages 36–37) to appear as you want it by controlling the size, weight, typeface and position of the text. The idea of formatting whole paragraphs is similar – you can apply a set of formatting rules to each paragraph to decide how it looks. The features you can control include the spacing above and below paragraphs, the amount of space between individual lines in a paragraph and the positions of the left and right margins.

● Visual appeal

The ability to control these aspects of paragraph formatting can come in handy, especially for longer documents or publications, such as newsletters. For example, you can make a newsletter more visually appealing if you apply formatting to the paragraphs of each article within it. Also, long documents such as reports often have different sections that require different treatments (introductions, appendixes, indexes and so forth). It's just

a case of thinking about what would work best for your target audience and then using the right formatting tools to achieve it.

● Reading between the lines

For example, if you were writing a play, you would want to make the script as easy as possible for the actors to follow. With this in mind, you might decide to make the left and right margins wide so that the paragraphs are narrower than on a normal document, making the lines easy to scan without losing your place.

Another example could be if you were writing a set of notes for students. You might decide to put plenty of space between the lines within each paragraph to make the information easier to follow and to provide room for the students or tutors to write in their own notes and comments.

Changes and corrections can be difficult and messy to make in handwritten work, but your PC can ensure that your documents are clear and easy to read when you use the formatting paragraphs facility.

PC TIPS

Triple-clicking

By now you'll be aware of how often you need to double-click your mouse to do certain things. For example, you can double-click to open an icon, file or folder in Windows; equally you can use the technique to highlight (and so select) a word in Word. Triple-clicking is a related technique where you click the mouse button three times in rapid succession to select a whole paragraph.

All the paragraph formatting options can be controlled via Word's Paragraph dialog box. First, you need to select the paragraph you want to format by using the drag-select technique to highlight it (or you could follow our PC Tips about triple-clicking, left). Call up the Paragraph dialog box by selecting Paragraph from the Format menu and then select the Indents and Spacing tab.

If you want to move the left and right margins, it's simply a question of using the up and down arrows to alter the values in the Left and Right text boxes found in the Indentation section. In addition, you can indent the first line of a paragraph further by using the Special text box in the Indentation section (see page 42).

● Making space

The Spacing section is used to control the spacing above and below a paragraph, as well as the spaces between the lines of a paragraph. You can use the Before and After text boxes to determine how big a space appears above and below a paragraph.

The Line spacing text box allows you to specify how much space there should be between the lines of a paragraph. The default is one line (Single). Word gives the options of one-and-a-half lines or double-spacing, as well as the extra flexibility to set an exact spacing distance. This spacing is measured in **points** (by default) and you can put whatever values you want in the At text box.

● Sneak preview

The Indents and Spacing tab in the Paragraph dialog box includes a preview facility that gives you some idea of what your paragraph formatting changes will look like before you click the OK button. The Preview screen automatically changes to show the alterations you made to the settings in the dialog box.

There is no need to format each individual paragraph of a document separately – unless you want to for style reasons. To format all the text, select your whole document by choosing Select All from the Edit menu and apply the same formatting to all the paragraphs in your document at once.

WHAT IT MEANS

POINTS

A point is the most common unit of measurement in printing. A point (often shortened to 'pt') is $^1/_{72}$ of an inch. For example, the text in this box is 8pt, the main text on this page is 10pt and the heading on page 40, 'Perfect paragraphs', is 67pt.

Your written documents will be easier to work on, easier to read and will convey a much more professional image when you format them in Word.

Changing margins and paragraph indents

Word provides a range of tools to help you improve the look of your text documents and make them more inviting for the reader. Here's our guide to margin and paragraph indents.

1 Below is the Print Layout view of the first few paragraphs of a long text document. Without paragraph formatting, the text looks daunting to the reader, so we're going to change the left and right margins for the whole document to shorten the lines.

2 To do this, we first need to select all the text in the letter by going to the Edit menu and choosing the Select All option. All the selected text will be shown as white text on a black background (as in Step 3).

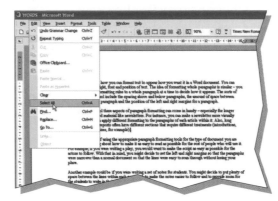

3 All the paragraph margin and indentation options are controlled via the Paragraph dialog box. To open this, go to the Format menu and click over the Paragraph option.

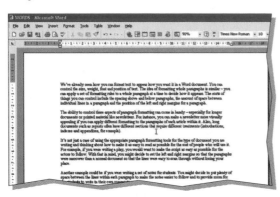

4 Click on the Indents and Spacing tab in the Paragraph dialog box. Let's start by moving the left margin in a bit. In the Left text box below the Indentation heading, click the up arrow to its right until the box reads 1.5cm. Notice how the bold text in the Preview window moves. Now do the same for the right margin. In the Right text box below the Indentation heading, click the up arrow until the box reads 1.5cm. You'll see the right end of the bold text move in the Preview window.

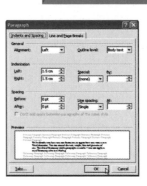

5 Click the OK button to see the changes. View the text normally by clicking once in the main window to make the highlight disappear. Look at the ruler at the top of the page – you will see the two sliders showing the new positions of the margins.

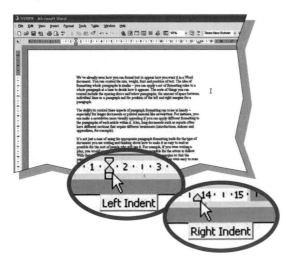

Left Indent

Right Indent

6 Now we're going to add indentations to the first line of each paragraph. First, you need to select all the text – go to the Edit menu and choose Select All. Now select Paragraph from the Format menu to open the Paragraph dialog box again. Click on the down arrow to the right of the Special text box and select First line from the list of options that appears. Notice how the measurement 1.27cm (it might be 0.3in on your PC) appears automatically in the By text box. Now click on the OK button and the result should be altogether more attractive and easier to read, as shown in the page on the right.

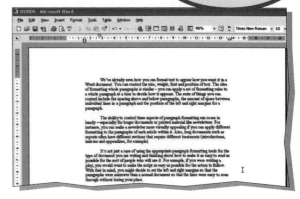

Giving your document space

Documents are often easier to read if the space between the lines of text is increased. Let's see how easy it is to do this.

1 Our document is formatted with margin and first line indents, but it still seems dense and difficult to read. Let's give it an airier look by increasing the space between the lines of text. Go to the Edit menu and choose the Select All option. Now choose the Paragraph option from the Format menu. In the Paragraph dialog box, locate the Line spacing text box, click on the down arrow to its right and select the Double option from the drop-down menu.

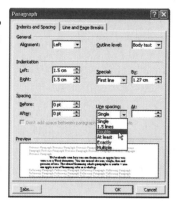

2 Click on OK and then click once on the document to see it with double line spacing. The text is much more legible. It's worth thinking about applying double line spacing to documents such as essays, where presentation is particularly important, and space may be needed for the teacher to make marks and comments.

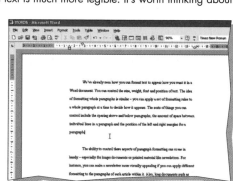

3 Word gives you a variety of line-spacing options, of which we chose Double in Step 1. However, you can choose the line spacing to suit your own preferences. To do this, select all the text, go to the Format menu, select Paragraph and choose Exactly from the Line spacing drop-down menu. Type in the space you want (this is measured in points, which is shortened to 'pt') in the At text box. We have selected a depth of 14pt.

4 When you click OK and then click on the text, you will see that the lines have closed up a little but the text is still legible. This paragraph formatting feature gives you great flexibility when you're working with different typefaces and type sizes, so you can create exactly the type of document presentation you are looking for.

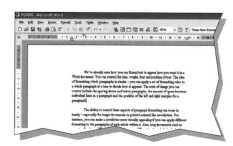

5 When you are writing Word documents, the usual way to create space between paragraphs is to press the [Enter] key twice. This creates an invisible character called a carriage return. You can make these characters visible by clicking on the Show/Hide button on Word's toolbar (inset).

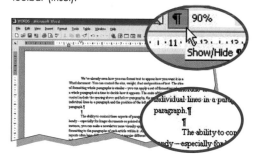

6 In the same way as you can change the spaces between lines, you can adjust the spacing between paragraphs. To do this, delete the extra carriage returns between the paragraphs of your document, then click on the Select All option from the Edit menu. Open the Paragraph dialog box. Click on the up arrow to the right of the Before text box in the Spacing section. Here we put a 6pt space (about half a line) above each of the paragraphs. The After box puts a 6pt space below each paragraph.

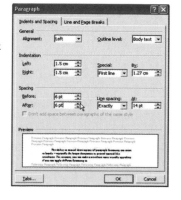

7 When you're happy with the changes you've made, click on the OK button to finish. Even on screen, the document shows that a lot of thought has been put into its presentation by the changes we've made to the paragraph formatting and line spacing.

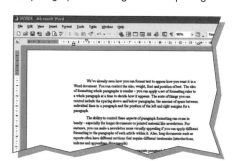

PC TIPS

At any time in the paragraph formatting process, it is possible to back-track by clicking on the Undo button on the toolbar (inset). Even if you've made several changes, you'll have the option of undoing them all.

Number your pages

Almost every long printed document, book or magazine has page numbers. You can manually add page numbers to your Word documents, but there's a much smarter automatic way.

It's no coincidence that almost every printed item you see has page numbers – books, magazines and newspapers all have them because they help readers to navigate through large amounts of written material and, with an index, make it easy to find exactly the right information. So, it's a good idea to add page numbers to your Word documents – especially if you ever need to write long reports or letters.

One way to include page numbers in a document is to manually type them in at the top or bottom of every page. This has the virtue of simplicity, but it can be pretty tiresome and time-consuming because you have to do it for every single page. In addition, you will have to check that you type in the correct number for each page and position the number in the same place on every page.

The biggest problem with inserting page numbers manually comes when you decide to modify your document by adding or removing text or even whole pages. Then you'll have to go right through your document and renumber all the pages and make sure text changes haven't shunted your page numbers away from their intended positions at the top or bottom of each page.

● Head and foot with ease

Word makes it easy to avoid these difficulties by creating **headers and footers** for documents, which offer three time-saving advantages. First, they are kept separate from the main text of your document so their position can't be altered by modifications you make to the rest of your document. Second, you only have to set up a header or footer for one page and Word will automatically apply it to all the pages in your document. And third, if the changes you make to the main document change the number of pages, Word automatically updates the page numbers in the headers and footers to cope with it.

Word gives you a toolbar to control the contents of headers and footers. You can access it by selecting Header and Footer from the View menu. Then it's a simple matter of typing whatever text you want to appear in the header or footer and clicking on the Close button on the toolbar.

Numbering the pages of your documents will help you and other readers to keep them in sequence.

Adding headers and footers

When you're working with lengthy documents, headers and footers can help you keep track of where you are and – when printed out – add professional polish to your work.

1 It's easy to add automatic page numbers to your long Word documents (our example is four pages long). First, open the Header and Footer toolbar, which controls what is inserted automatically at the top and bottom of every page in a document. To do this, go to the View menu and select the Header and Footer option.

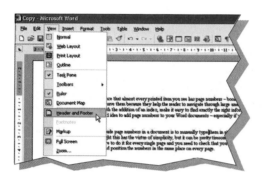

2 Now you can see the Header and Footer toolbar and a dotted rectangle that shows where the header is positioned on the page. To insert the correct page number automatically on all pages of the document, click over the Insert Page Number button (it has a # on it).

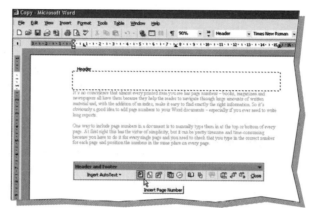

3 You can format text in the header in the same way as you format normal text in a document. Here we have centred the number '1' in the header box by clicking over the Center button in the main toolbar.

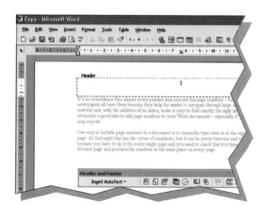

4 When you've finished work on the header, click on the Close button to close the Header and Footer toolbar and return to Word's normal document-editing mode. The header box disappears – it still exists, but Word has just hidden it so that it doesn't distract you.

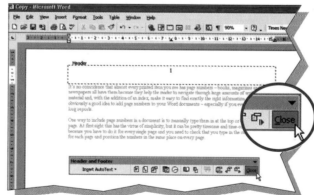

5 To see what your finished document looks like with page numbers in place before you save or print it, you must be in the Print Layout view (if necessary, select Print Layout from the View menu). Notice how the page number in the header is shown in grey.

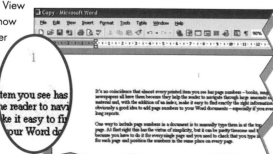

6 If you want to have the page numbers at the foot of the page instead of the head, click on the Switch Between Header and Footer icon (inset) in the Header and Footer toolbar. You'll then see a Footer box at the bottom of the page. You can insert the page number and format this footer in the same way as the header (see Steps 2 and 3).

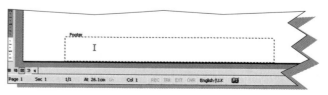

Switch Between Header and Footer

Microsoft® Word

PC TIPS

Header and footer extras

Your headers and footers need not be limited to page numbers. If you click on the Insert AutoText button on the Header and Footer toolbar,

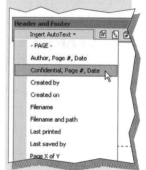

you'll see a drop-down menu with a range of options that you can include at the head or foot of every page of your document, such as Confidential, Page #, Date.

Styles made easy

Word's formatting tools are great, but changing typefaces, type sizes and adding bold and underlining can quickly become a chore – especially on a long document. Use Word's styles to make changes quickly and easily.

One of Word's best features is its huge variety of formatting commands. In previous exercises we've seen how selecting words and paragraphs in your letters and then clicking on Word's buttons and menus to change type styles and formats allows you to personalize your documents, making them easier to read (see Stage 1, pages 36–37 and 40–41).

Over time, you will find that you develop your favourite combinations of formatting options. For example, you might like the main text of formal letters to use the Times New Roman typeface in 10 point, with one-and-a-half line spacing. You could use another typeface, size and spacing combination to make your name and address at the top of your letters look like a professional letterhead.

● **The hard way**
Although formatting text in Word is simple, applying these combinations quickly becomes repetitive, and the longer your document is, the more likely you are to make errors.

Imagine, for example, you wanted to change all the headings in your document. This could involve six different operations: you would have to select your text, convert it to your chosen typeface, change it to the required size, insert the desired space before each paragraph and then add bold and underlining. If you had to make each of these changes, it would take a lot of time and you might forget to make all the changes to all the headings.

● **The easy way**
Fortunately, Word provides a better way to make these frequent formatting changes, which is accessed through the Task Pane or the main Word toolbar. A number of features under the Styles and Formatting options allow you to make all these changes with one click of the mouse. At a stroke they cut out the tedious, repetitive work, so you need never worry about inconsistency in your documents because you forgot, for example, to add bold to some of the headings.

Word has a range of ready-made styles that are easy to use. By default, all documents you create are in the Normal style: 10 point Times New Roman with no extra formatting. To change the text style in your document, ensure the Task Pane panel is open (see pages 34–35) and the Styles and Formatting panel is displayed. Select the text with the mouse and click once on any of the options listed. Each style has a name, and the formatting commands it combines are shown in preview form so you can see what your text will look

Styles determine the look of text, main headings and sub-heads, as well as other parts of your document, such as list elements. You can set them up to look the way you want.

PC TIPS

Although styles are usually applied to paragraphs, you can also apply them to single words and phrases. For instance, if you highlight a word before selecting a style, Word will apply the style to that word only. If you don't highlight any text, Word applies the style to the paragraph that contains the text insertion point.

like before you make any changes. Alternatively, click on the arrow to the right of the styles (the default is Normal) on the Word toolbar and select a style from the drop-down list.

● **Your own style**

Word's built-in styles are fine, but if you find them unappealing or too restrictive, you can make your own, give them a name and they

will appear in the list of styles along with the other typefaces.

Word remembers the styles you created so the next time you start up your computer and open a document, your own styles will still be there, along with the others. This is particularly useful if you create lots of similar letters. By using styles, you remove the risk of inconsistencies creeping into a series of letters or documents.

Using Word's ready-made styles

Word has a set of styles that you can apply to any of the documents you create. With just a few clicks, you can dramatically change the look of your letters in seconds.

1 Here's a simple one-page letter containing a short list of three books. To draw attention to them, we want to treat the titles and authors as headings. We'll format them so they stand out more. We could select each heading and then click on several of Word's individual formatting buttons, such as Bold. However, to make several changes at once, we'll use Word's styles. First, put the text insertion point anywhere in the first heading.

2 If the Styles and Formatting panel is not displayed, click once on the small downward-pointing arrowhead next to the Task Pane title and select Styles and Formatting from the drop-down list. The range of styles available will be displayed under the Pick formatting to apply heading (inset).

3 Word conveniently shows the styles in preview form, so choosing a new look for the heading in your document is as simple as choosing the most appropriate one from the list shown. Pausing the mouse over a style brings up a box of useful information about the style, including any extra formatting (bold in this case) and the size of the typeface (16 point in this example).

4 Click once on your preferred style to apply it; in this case we have chosen Heading 1. This instantly improves the look and readability of the letter. It now becomes much more professional in its appearance.

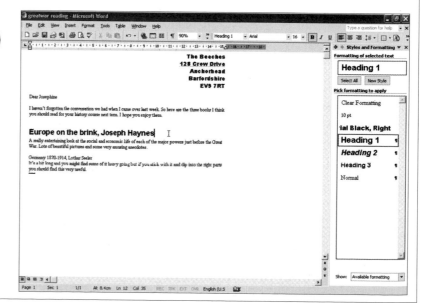

Creating your own styles

You might find Word's ready-made styles a little dull for some letters, but you can very easily create your own. Here's how to give your documents a personal look.

1 Creating your own style is as easy as telling Word what combination of formatting you want and giving it a name. Start by selecting the Styles and Formatting option from the Task Pane.

2 The Styles and Formatting panel appears. Initially, there are only a few styles listed (inset). Click on New Style to open the New Style dialog box.

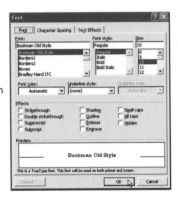

STYLES FROM TEXT

If you already have a document containing text that you have formatted by hand – using Word's individual format commands – you can quickly create styles straight from the text.

Open a document and place the text insertion point in the text that has already been formatted by hand. Open the Task Pane and you will see it in the list, even though you may not have had the Task Pane open at the time of formatting.

In fact, each style in your document will appear in the Task Pane, even if you haven't created it as a style, as Word tracks each instance of formatting and places it in the Task Pane as you type.

You can give this style a name by clicking on the arrow next to it, selecting Modify Style and typing in a name in the Modify Style dialog box which appears. The new name of the style will now appear in your list of styles for that document.

3 Type in a name for your style. We've chosen 'My text style'. Leave the other options as they are and click on the Format button in the bottom-left corner. A list of options will appear (inset). Choose Font to start specifying the appearance of the text in your style.

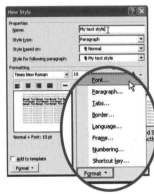

4 This is the usual Word Font dialog box. We've chosen Bookman Old Style in 10 point size for our text. Once you've made your choices, press the OK button to return to the New Style dialog box.

5 Click on the Format button again, but this time select the Paragraph option from the pop-up list.

6 This is the standard Paragraph dialog box (see pages 40–43). Here you can adjust the space between lines and the way text behaves when it reaches the end of a line. We've chosen a justified alignment, a 1.27cm (½ in) indentation for the first line of each paragraph, line spacing of Exactly 13 points and a space of 6 points before each paragraph. Choose your options and then click on OK.

7 Now you will see the elements of your style listed under the Preview section; the combined effects are also shown in the Preview. Click on the OK button.

8 Your new style is now listed in the Task Pane, along with the original styles. Pausing your mouse over it brings up the specification of your style. You can also now choose your style from the styles list on the main toolbar.

9 Applying the new style to text is as simple as using one of Word's built-in styles. Type in some text. Place the text insertion point in the paragraph and select My text style from the list of styles in the Task Pane window (inset). The instant result is shown far right.

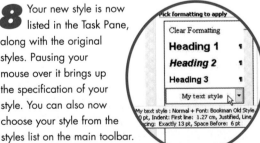

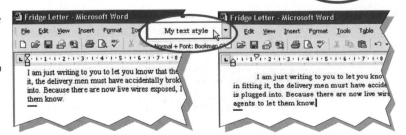

Getting more from styles

Here are some useful techniques for getting the most out of your text styles.

WORD'S STYLES are powerful tools to help minimize the time and effort you spend making your documents look good, leaving you free to concentrate on the actual words. To really get the most out of Word's styles, there are a few options that are worth trying. First, if you want your style to be available in all your documents, tick the Add to template option before you press the OK button on the New Style or Modify Style dialog box.

You might find that you want to change a style you've already created – perhaps because you've just added a new typeface that you want to use. Click on the small arrowhead to the right of the style. Select Modify from the drop-down list and you can change any aspect you want from the Modify Style dialog box. The next step is to add special keyboard shortcuts to format your documents (see below).

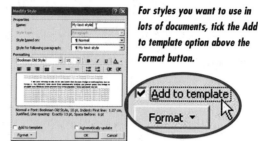

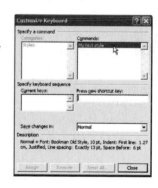

For styles you want to use in lots of documents, tick the Add to template option above the Format button.

You can change a style from the Task Pane at any time by clicking on the arrow by the style to open the drop-down menu and then selecting Modify.

Assigning styles from the keyboard

Once you have created your favourite styles, you can use them to greater effect by assigning them a keyboard shortcut of their own. Here's how to do it.

1 When creating a new style (or modifying an existing style), choose Shortcut key from the pop-up Format menu in the New Style or Modify Style dialog box.

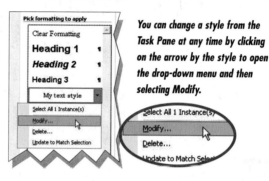

2 The Customize Keyboard dialog box pops up. You can see the style you are working on (here, it is the My text style we created on the opposite page). The cursor is flashing in the Press new shortcut key text box.

We need to find a keyboard shortcut that isn't already being used. For example, Word uses [Ctrl]+[C] as a shortcut for selecting the Copy option from the Edit menu.

3 Try typing in [Ctrl]+[C]. The shortcut appears but Word tells you that this is already assigned. Press the [Backspace] key until the text box is empty again.

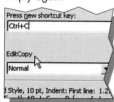

4 Try pressing [Ctrl]+[Shift]+[1]. Word interprets this as [Ctrl]+[!] and tells us that this keyboard shortcut is not taken, so you can click on the Assign button.

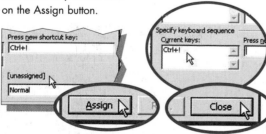

5 You will see your new keyboard shortcut listed in the Current keys text box. Click on Close.

6 Click on the OK button in your New Style or Modify Style dialog box and return to your document. Now, place the text insertion point in a paragraph of text and press the [Ctrl]+[Shift]+[1] keyboard shortcut. You will see the paragraph immediately change to the formatting contained in the My text style. Any new text that you key in will appear in the My text style until you select a new style.

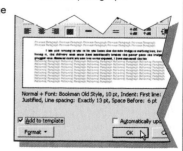

Basic typography

With so many fonts to choose from, a computer user can fall into the trap of making a page look confusing and difficult to read. However, you can avoid this by learning the basics of typography.

Typography – the art of choosing and using typefaces – has changed radically with the arrival of computers, modern word processors and desktop publishing. At least, its ease of use has changed. The laborious process of using individual metal blocks for each letter has been replaced by quick, clean and easy electronic processes. Today, you can change the size of all the text on your page with a keystroke. Previously, a small army of typesetters had to rebuild the whole page physically using thousands of letter blocks – a time-consuming and very expensive process.

● Swings and roundabouts

Such flexibility does have a slight downside as it's very easy to take typography for granted, ignoring (or being ignorant of) the principles that have been honed over generations. The result is often a page that would make a classically trained designer blush.

Not that design shouldn't be different and adventurous – far from it. However, a working knowledge of the occasions when it's appropriate to be different and adventurous and when it's not will help you to produce more effective and legible pages.

So what are the basics of typography? Well, for starters, the most obvious difference between fonts (typefaces) is that some are serif (which have tiny flourishes at the ends of each stroke of a letter) and some are sans serif (which don't have flourishes). You can see the flourishes very clearly on the big letter T in the first paragraph on this page; the heading is a sans serif font and has no flourishes at all.

● Serif or sans serif?

Serif fonts have an elegant, authoritative feel, partly because they have been around for so many years. Serif fonts are also easier to read, as the serifs create lines that hold the eye. They are therefore well suited for smaller text, such as the main 'body' text in a letter, magazine or newspaper.

A sans serif font, however, imparts a sense of modernity and 'arty' fashionability. Sans serif fonts are harder to follow, so they are less commonly used for body text. When they are, the font tends to be a bit bigger and more widely spaced in order to make it easier to read. It will probably be part of a more 'airy' page, with lots of white space around other items on the page, too. As a result, the word count per page will be significantly lower than

Although it looks good for special effects, mixing and matching fonts is rarely a good idea – the page is unsettling to look at and words are not so easy to make out.

Microsoft® Word

with a serif font. Again, sans serif fonts are well suited for arty publications, where the pictures and overall look matter most.

Headlines, logos and slogans, such as those found on advertisements, provide much greater freedom in font selection because they are larger and so legibility is less of an issue. However, the increased size of such 'display text' presents its own range of problems because small details become so much more obvious (see page 53). For very small amounts of text, such as in logos, designers may well create their own typeface, or customize an existing font, to create a unique look.

● Read all about it

Owing to the varying suitability of fonts, many publications choose to mix and match, with sans serif display text and serif body text – the most obvious and influential example being *The Guardian* newspaper. Have a look at a front page and note the difference between the dense body copy and the spacious display text. Compare this with a more traditional newspaper, such as *The Daily Telegraph*, which is much 'busier' and tends to

have a greater mixture of different items on each page. As a general rule, unless you have a specific reason to do otherwise, try not to include more than two fonts on a single page. Less, in this case, is definitely more.

● Styles within styles

There seem to be countless different fonts, and their variety can be daunting at first. However, classic typefaces fall into only a handful of categories, which have developed in the 500 or so years since the invention of the printing press.

Each style can have several different examples and these may be further subdivided into different weights (bold, extra bold or 'black'), or different widths (narrow or condensed and expanded), but the same general rules apply. There are also various specialist fonts, such as the script-style Embassy (used for wedding invitations, for example), typewriter-style fonts, such as Courier (which was particularly trendy at the end of the 1990s), plus a host of weird and wonderful one-offs. The box below will give you some pointers for effective font usage.

Know your fonts

Here we introduce you to some of the fonts that have become popular since the invention of the printing press.

BEING PRESENTED with a font list for the first time can be daunting as there are so many typefaces. However, most classic fonts fall into a handful of categories or are just variations on other fonts.

Fonts have developed over time, as improved printing techniques have allowed typefaces to become subtler and

Isabella

Garamond has rounded serifs and is a tasteful and classic font.

more precise. The oldest (actually called Old Style) tend not to have much difference between thick and thin strokes and have quite rounded serifs – **Garamond** is a good example. Such fonts gradually became more developed until they ended up with an appearance such as **Bodoni**, which is quite heavy and formal-looking and has major differences between the thick and thin strokes. It is also completely vertical with very straight serifs and no bracketing (i.e. curve) between the serif and the main part of the letter. You'd have to take a deep breath before you approached a page of Bodoni: it's more suited to formal publications and

Sir John

Bodoni is a much more formal font, ideally suited to important official documents.

documents and only then, ideally, as display type. Bodoni was something of a natural typographical conclusion, after which type became more esoteric,

Harold

Century (Old Style) is great to use when clarity is needed.

deriving its influences from wider sources. This led to 'Egyptian-style' faces, with thick, slab-like serifs, less contrast between thick and thin strokes and generally a very simple appearance. A good example is **Century**. Its boldness makes it a good display type, and it is very popular for children's books because of its simplicity and legibility.

Finally, there are the contemporary faces, such as **Helvetica**, the classic sans serif font, which only really came into its own in the 1960s. This is a very 'clean' design, that's readable in larger type sizes and has a very contemporary look and feel.

Mrs Smith

Helvetica is one of the simple sans serif fonts that seems to survive the vagaries of fashion.

The range of fonts supplied with Windows and Word is more than enough to get you started, but you might like to install others as you become more typographically aware.

Adding a drop capital

A drop capital, often called a 'drop cap', is a classic way of livening up text. Word automates the process, but you can tweak the effect manually for more satisfying results.

1 We'll start by adding a drop capital to the first paragraph in a newsletter. Type in some suitable text and turn the document into a multi-column format by using the Columns button on the toolbar (inset).

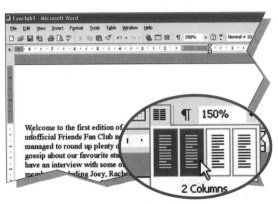

2 Make sure the text cursor is within the first paragraph and then click on the Format menu and select Drop Cap from the list of options.

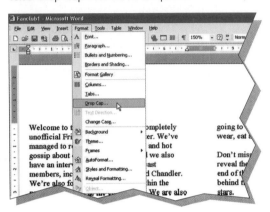

3 The Drop Cap dialog box will appear. The first of the small pictures will be selected, indicating normal text. Click on the middle picture (inset).

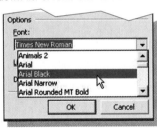

4 You'll see that the lower part of the dialog box, labelled Options, which was greyed out before, is now 'live'. Click on the downward-pointing arrow under Font to access the drop-down list of fonts and select a different one. We've chosen Arial Black to provide a good contrast to the main text in the paragraph, which is still Times New Roman. Click on the OK button.

5 Word now inserts a ready-made text box that contains the first letter of the paragraph (which has also been automatically removed from the paragraph text itself). The rest of the paragraph text runs around the drop cap letter – just as in a newspaper or magazine story.

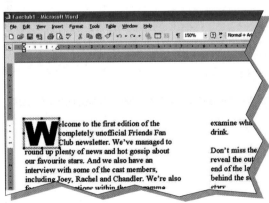

6 Now all you have to do is click anywhere else in the Word document to see what the paragraph looks like without the outline.

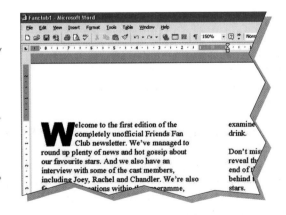

Adjusting spacing on headline text

When you start to handle display type or headlines there are different things to consider than when you are using a smaller type size.

1 We've started with a single headline, changing the font size to 60 points so that it almost fills the page. We've also centred the headline and added some rules above and below the text using the Borders and Shading option under the Format menu to make it stand out. However, there are some problems that appear when text is increased to such a size: there's a little too much space between most of the letters and there's far too much space between the 'W' and 'a', whereas the 'r' and 't' are almost touching.

2 To change the individual letter spacing we will have to adjust the **kerning**. Select all the text in the headline, using the mouse to highlight it, and then select the Font option from the Format menu.

3 The Font dialog box appears. Click on the Character Spacing tab to access the options that control the amount of space between the letters. You'll see your selected text in the Preview panel at the bottom of the dialog box.

4 The second line of options in the dialog box is labelled Spacing. This lets you specify how much the text is squeezed together or pulled apart. Click on the small downward-pointing arrow head next to the By text box. The first time you click, you'll see the Spacing text box change to read Condensed, and the By text box will read 0.1 pt. Keep pressing the arrow head until it reads 1 pt. Then click on OK.

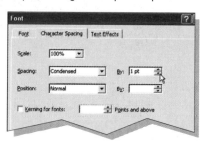

KERNING

Sometimes the default values for the gaps between the characters of a font are too large or (more rarely) too small. When you tighten or loosen these gaps by the same value across a body of text it is called tracking.

However, there are some occasions when the problem exists only between a couple of letters: common examples include AT, AV, Te, Yo and LY, to name just a few. The gap between two letters can be adjusted and this is called kerning.

5 You'll see your headline is now a little tighter, although there's still too much space between the 'W' and the 'a'. Select the 'W' on its own.

6 Bring up the Character Spacing tab of the Font dialog box again. This time, type a larger figure directly into the By text box. Here we have put 8 pt. Then press the OK button.

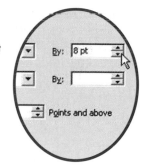

7 You'll now see that the first two letters of the headline look much better and the 'W' no longer appears to be on its own.

8 Look more closely at the rest of the letter spacing and repeat the exercise where necessary. For example, to make sure the 'r' and the 't' don't touch in our example, we expanded the spacing by 2 pt.

9 Once you've been through the headline, you'll have a design that looks a lot better than the original way Word displayed the text. You need only do this trial-and-error spacing for large text sizes and, with a little practice, you'll soon find it easy to get rid of unsightly gaps.

Copying and pasting cell contents

It's essential to be able to copy and paste information in Windows programs. Here we show you how easy it is to use this technique to transfer text and numbers between cells in Excel.

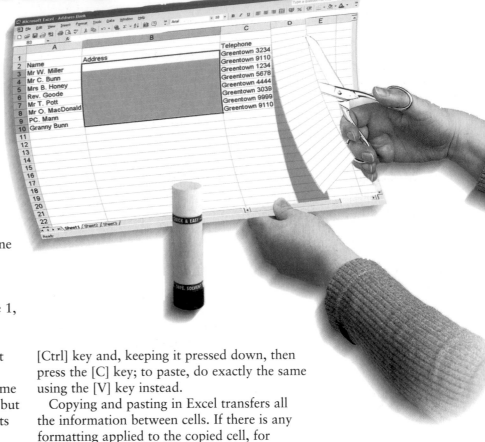

Techniques that allow you to cut and copy text or numbers from one place and paste them somewhere else are extremely useful. We've seen how you can save time by cutting, copying and pasting text in Word (see Stage 1, pages 16–17) and parts of pictures in Paint (see Stage 1, pages 74–75), and the same techniques can be used in Excel to copy text and numbers between spreadsheet cells.

Copying and pasting in Excel can be as time saving as it is in other Windows programs, but it also has the added bonus that spreadsheets often contain numerical data, which is essential to move accurately. You can't be certain of avoiding mistakes if you retype data in cells, but copying and pasting – when done correctly – is always accurate.

● Select the cell
The first step of a copy and paste operation is to select the cell whose contents you wish to copy. To do this, click on the cell and a thick black rectangle will appear around it. Next, copy the cell's contents by going to the Edit menu and choosing the Copy option.

Now you need to select the cell where you want to paste the information. You select this cell by using the same technique as you used to select the first cell – click on it. Finally, paste the information by going to the Edit menu and choosing the Paste option.

There are keyboard shortcuts for the copy and paste operations. To copy, press the

[Ctrl] key and, keeping it pressed down, then press the [C] key; to paste, do exactly the same using the [V] key instead.

Copying and pasting in Excel transfers all the information between cells. If there is any formatting applied to the copied cell, for example, the background colour of a cell, the colour of text or numbers and their typeface and size, it will also be transferred to the cell where you paste.

Copying and pasting addresses

The advantage of copying and pasting the contents of cells in Excel is that all the other information – formatting and formulae – are copied as well as words and numbers.

PC TIPS

Quick copy to adjacent cells

You may want to copy text or numbers to the next cell across or down. In Excel, there is a quick way to do this.

Select the cell from which you want to copy. A black box appears around it with a small black square at the corner. Position the mouse over this square, and the pointer changes to

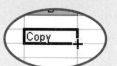

a small black cross; press and drag the cursor across until the next cell is selected. Release the mouse button. The text or

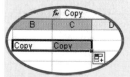

numeric contents of the cell will be copied into the adjacent cell. A small box appears in the corner of the new cell which gives you various options – to copy only the cell content or the fomatting too.

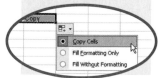

6 Now let's see what happens when we copy from a cell with a coloured background and different-coloured text. Click on the cell that contains Ms T. Pott's address (cell B7) and then press the [Ctrl] + [C] keys to copy this cell's contents.

1 In this example, we've started work on a new Excel spreadsheet to use as an address book. We've already included Mr Bunn the baker and now we're adding Granny Bunn, who lives at the same address. To save the effort of typing the address again, we'll just copy and paste it.

2 We want to copy Mr Bunn's address, so select the cell that contains the address by clicking on it. Notice how a thick black border appears around this cell to remind you that it is the currently selected cell. You can also see that its contents are shown in the Formula bar.

3 The next step is to take a copy of Mr Bunn's address. To do this, you have to go to the Edit menu and select the Copy option. As with all other Windows programs, the keyboard shortcut in Excel for copying is to press the [Ctrl] key and, keeping it pressed down, press the [C] key.

4 As a reminder, Excel has now put a flashing dotted line around the cell that contains the address we've just copied. The next step is to select the cell into which we want to paste this address. Do this simply by clicking on the relevant cell (in this case, cell B10). The thick black border appears around this cell.

5 Now let's paste in the address. To do this, go to the Edit menu and select the Paste option. Don't forget that, as with other Windows programs, the keyboard shortcut in Excel for pasting is to press the [Ctrl] key and, with it pressed down, then the [V] key.

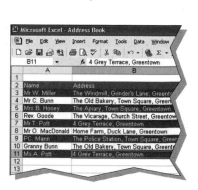

7 Paste this address into cell B11 by selecting the cell and using the keyboard shortcut of pressing the [Ctrl] + [V] keys. Next, press the [Enter] key to dismiss the flashing dotted line from around cell B7. Notice how this has transferred the text and cell background colours as well as the actual words.

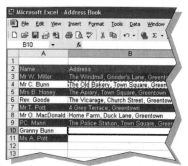

Printing spreadsheets

Once you've created a spreadsheet, you will usually want to print it out. But what if it has so many columns that it won't fit on the page? Don't worry, Excel has features that help you to produce printed spreadsheets – regardless of their width or length.

When it comes to printing, an Excel spreadsheet is a different kind of document to one created in a word processor, such as Microsoft Word. With Word, you can carry on typing as long as you wish. When you have filled up one page, the text carries on to the next, as in a book. The width of the text is usually set to fit on the printed page, although if you want to change the amount of text you can move the margins to make columns wider or narrower.

It's much the same when it comes to printing. Microsoft Word treats the document as a collection of pages, with left and right margins, and prints as many pages as are required for the length of the text. If you need to print wide columns of text, you can tell the word processor to print out in landscape format, sideways across the page

(see pages 94–95), instead of the usual portrait format with the page upright.

● **Printing irregular documents**
Spreadsheets in Excel are different, however, as an Excel worksheet can be both long and wide. It is easy to print a small worksheet that is only a few columns wide and not too many rows long, but a worksheet can quickly become too large to fit on a single page.

To overcome this, Excel divides the worksheet into sections that fit the paper in your printer and prints each section on a separate page. Alternatively, if you don't need the whole worksheet, you can print out the part you need on a single page.

To see how this works, let's look at a worksheet showing household expenditure (opposite), which you might want to print out to show to members of the family.

PC TIPS

Print Preview
Like Microsoft Word, Excel has a Print Preview option to let you see how your worksheet will print before you send it to the printer (see Step 2, opposite). It's a particularly useful option in Excel, since sometimes you might want to print only a section of a larger worksheet.

Printing your chart

We saw how to enter data and create a pie chart in Stage 1 on pages 60–61. Here, we'll show you how to print out the chart so that it fits perfectly onto the page.

PC TIPS

Page breaks

When you have a large worksheet that won't fit onto one sheet of paper, Excel sets automatic page breaks so that it can be printed on several sheets. If you only need part of a worksheet to fit on one page, you can insert a manual page break to show Excel where you want to start printing.

Suppose you want to print from the part of the worksheet that

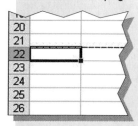

begins at cell A22. First, select cell A22 by clicking on it to highlight it, then click on the Insert menu. Select Page Break from the menu and a dotted line will appear above row 22 to indicate the start of the new page.

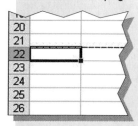

1 Type in some categories and numbers and use the Chart Wizard tool (see Stage 1, page 61) to create a 3D pie chart on the right of your worksheet. Drag the borders of the chart so that it's prominent on the right-hand side of the page.

2 Click on the left-hand side of the page, where you have typed in the figures. Go to the File menu and select Print Preview. You will now see a view of how the worksheet would appear on an A4 page. Notice that the right-hand side of the chart is missing – it is too wide to fit across an A4 page in this upright (portrait) format. But it would fit if the paper was the other way round.

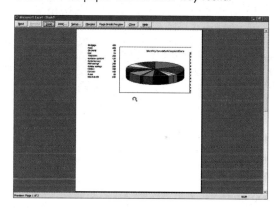

3 Click on the Close button on the toolbar above the page to close the Print Preview. Now click on Excel's File menu and select the Page Setup option. A dialog box will pop up to show you the settings that control how your Excel worksheet fits on the page.

4 You will see that there are two options displayed at the top of the dialog box, under the heading Orientation. These control which way round the page will appear on the printed paper. The two small page icons (containing the letter A) on the left of each option show the difference between portrait and landscape orientation. Click on the Landscape option and press the OK button to return to the worksheet.

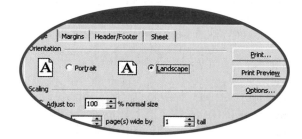

5 Now, when you select the Page Preview option from the File menu, you'll see how the worksheet fits on the page without being chopped off on the right-hand side. Of course, with landscape orientation, you get fewer lines on a page, but in this case that doesn't matter. If you can get into the habit of using Page Preview before you print your worksheets, you'll avoid wasting paper and time.

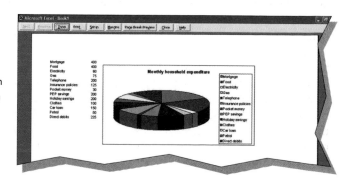

Adding or altering cells

O nce you have started to use your spreadsheet program, you might find that a better way of presenting the information comes to mind. Alternatively, you might come to realize that some of the information contained on the worksheet is unnecessary, while other figures or data need to be added.

When updating an existing worksheet, this will become even more apparent. For example, it is more than likely that the monthly household expenditure figures and categories needed for December will be very different to those required for April.

● Multiple changes
You can, of course, make changes to your worksheet at the level of individual cells. While this method is fine for small worksheets, it can be extremely laborious and time-consuming when you have a larger spreadsheet or when you want to make changes and improvements to a larger area. For example, if you are

No matter how well you plan your spreadsheet before creating it, you will inevitably need to make alterations as you go along. Fortunately, Excel makes it easy to move data around or add information to the worksheet.

keeping lists of house contents and prices for insurance purposes, you will want to update the figures. You might also find that you need to incorporate additional elements in your worksheet in order to adapt to your changing needs. For example, if you are keeping a club list, you might discover that you need to add a completely new column to reflect an additional club activity, or a new row to cover a new member.

As we'll see in the step-by-step example opposite, Excel allows you to add to or delete from your spreadsheet quickly and effectively.

Drag and drop your cells

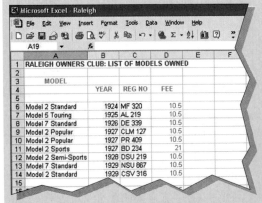

You can easily move an individual cell by using the mouse to drag and drop it. In the example above, the first category listed – 'Model' – is in the wrong row.

To move it to the correct position, click inside the cell to highlight it, then move the cursor to the edge of the cell. The normal cross-shaped cursor changes to an arrow pointer. Drag the cell down one position – you'll see the cell outline move – and drop the cell into place.

Updating your spreadsheet

In this step-by-step example, we use a cycle club membership spreadsheet to show how you can update information to accommodate changing circumstances.

IN THIS EXAMPLE, we have already given the worksheet some formatting by adding some different colours and centring the category headings in their various columns (see Stage 1, pages 58–59, for formatting details). Now we need to update some of the stored information. The first task is to record the receipts of an increased membership fee. After that, we need to add an entirely new column to the worksheet that will contain some additional information about the members. For this exercise, you can either type in the data shown in the example below, or use the same principles on a worksheet you've already created. They will apply equally well.

Microsoft® Excel

1 The club membership fees have increased, so we need to delete the old figures. Begin by moving the cursor over cell D6 and clicking inside it.

2 Holding down the left button, drag the mouse down to cell D14. The figures we want to delete will now be highlighted and appear on a blue background.

3 Press the [Delete] key (located on the keyboard to the right of [Enter]) to delete all the figures in the selected cells. The new membership figures can now be entered.

PC TIPS

Sometimes you will need to insert more than one column. For example, if you need two new columns between B and C, click on the column header to the right (C) and drag the mouse to highlight a second column (D). When you select Columns from the Insert menu, Excel will add the two new columns.

4 Now, imagine we want to include additional data, such as a column describing our members' bikes. To do this, we need to add a new column between existing columns A and B. Click on the header of the column that is to the right of where you want the new column (in this case, column B). The whole of column B is now highlighted. Click on the Insert menu and move the pointer down to highlight Columns.

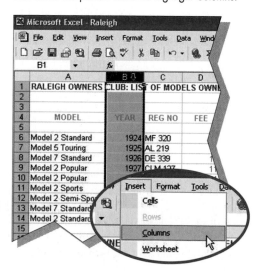

5 When you release the mouse button, Excel inserts a new blank column to the right of column A. The old column B moves to the right and is renamed column C. The new column B will be the same width as the column to its left (column A). We can make this narrower if we want (see Stage 1, pages 58–59) before typing in the new heading and data to complete the update.

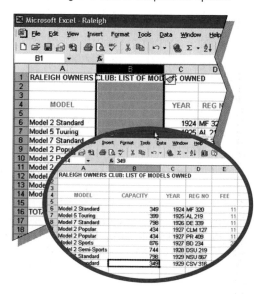

Quick calculations

Back in Stage 1, we learnt to use Excel to type in data, perform calculations with that data and present the formulae and results in a spreadsheet. However, Excel is just as useful for those times when you want to make a quick, *ad hoc* calculation on a set of figures, such as working out an astronomy problem for homework. In fact, Excel's powerful features make it a much more flexible tool than using pen, paper and a calculator.

The secret of using Excel to do on-the-spot calculations is that it provides an easy-to-use built-in tool for working out common functions without even having to type in a formula. This tool is called AutoCalculate and its default (and most obvious) function is Sum, which adds up a set of numbers.

● Summing it up

Here's how to use it. Imagine that you have typed the numbers '45', '44', '2', '656' and '7878' into cells C2, C3, C4, C5 and C6 of your worksheet and that you want to know quickly what they add up to. To start, all you have to do is click and drag the mouse to highlight and select the cells. Then look in the Status bar at the bottom of your Excel window. In one of the beige boxes on the right-hand side, you will see text that reads Sum=8625 (see far right below). This is the result you were looking for and all you had to do was highlight the relevant cells.

It is just as quick to perform other functions with AutoCalculate. These include: Average (which calculates the average of the figures in the selected cells); Count (which counts the number of cells selected); Count Nums (which tells you how many of the selected cells contain valid numbers); Max (which tells you the highest value number in the cells selected); and Min (which tells you the lowest value number in the cells selected).

If you want to set up AutoCalculate to display the result of one of these functions instead of Sum, you have to change the setting manually. For example, let's imagine now that you wanted to calculate the average of the five numbers in cells C2 to C6

Excel's formulae can be too time-consuming when you just want to work out a few figures. So here's the quick and easy way to get results with the AutoCalculate tool.

from our earlier example. The first step is to right-click on the Status bar to bring up the AutoCalculate options menu. Notice how Sum has a tick beside it. This indicates that it is the active function, but we want to change that, so click on Average to select it as the current function. Finally, go back and highlight cells C2 to C6 and you will see the text Average=1725 appear in a beige box in the Status bar.

AutoCalculate's default setting is Sum, which adds up a selected column or row of numbers.

Making the most of AutoCalculate

AutoCalculate can be useful when you want to do several quick calculations on a set of figures without the bother of creating formulae. Here's an astronomical example.

1 Here is some data about Jupiter's moons that we're going to analyze as part of a homework project. Let's imagine that we wanted to find the total of all the radii of orbit of Jupiter's moons. One way to work it out would be to put a formula in cell C21. We've already seen how to use the AutoSum tool in Stage 1, pages 62–63, and the formula we would need to type in is '=SUM (C5:C20)'. When you press [Enter], the result appears in cell C21.

2 However, writing formulae can be tedious and we might want to work out several different things about the radii of orbit. Instead, we could use the AutoCalculate tool. First delete the contents of cell C21 and highlight all the radii of orbit (cells C5 to C20). Now if you look towards the bottom right of the screen, you'll see the result has appeared in the Status bar: Sum= 141,736.20. By default, AutoCalculate shows the sum of the numbers you have selected.

PENCIL AND PAPER

When you highlight a row or column of numbers, the AutoCalculate facility adds up the numbers and shows their sum in the Status bar. However, as soon as you click on another cell in your spreadsheet, the result will disappear from the Status bar. For this reason it's a good idea to keep a pencil and piece of paper handy when you're using AutoCalculate so that you can write down the results as you go.

AutoCalculate Record
Sum of radiuses of orbit of Jupiter's moons
141,736,200

3 Now let's try to work out the average radius of orbit for Jupiter's moons. As above, we could place a formula in cell C21, but we have to use another function to calculate the average rather than the SUM function. So the formula we need to type in is '=AVERAGE (C5:C20)'. When you press the [Enter] key, the result appears in cell C21.

4 Luckily, average is also one of the AutoCalculate functions. First delete the contents of C21. Next we have to tell the tool to switch from working out the sum to working out the average. To do this, simply right-click anywhere in the Status bar and select Average from the menu that appears.

5 Now it's easy to see the average of the radii of orbit. Just use the drag-select technique with your mouse to highlight all the radius of orbit data and the result will appear in the Status bar where it says Average=8,858.51.

6 AutoCalculate also includes functions that calculate the highest and lowest figures from a selected set of cells. To use these functions, right-click on the Status bar and choose Max (for the highest figure) or Min (for the lowest figure). Then highlight the cells to which you want to apply it. The result appears in the Status bar.

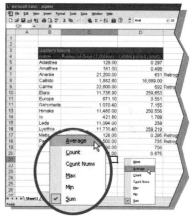

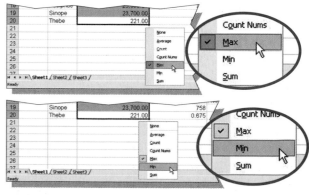

Introducing Excel's Task Panes

This panel of options lets you issue many common commands with a single click and has the space to provide helpful guidance that Excel's menus and toolbars cannot.

There are three methods for issuing commands to Excel: clicking on the words on the menu bar and selecting from menu options, clicking on toolbar buttons or typing a keyboard shortcut. Each method has its strengths and weaknesses. For instance, the single-click toolbar buttons are perfect – if you can recall what each button does without having to wait for the tooltip to tell you. Similarly, many people find keyboard shortcuts quick to carry out, but hard to remember. And the menus are a logical but often time-consuming means of working with Excel's functions.

If you haven't used Excel's Task Panes before, now is the time to put yourself in touch with the program's powerful commands – with just one click of the mouse.

● Enter the Task Pane

With the Office XP suite of programs – including Excel 2002 and Word 2002 – an additional method of issuing commands has been introduced. A Task Pane – in the form of a slim column – appears on the right of the screen and contains a list of commands that you can activate with a single click. The Office XP programmers have exploited the fact that many people now have large screens on their PCs, and don't mind sacrificing some space for a speedier, more user-friendly means of telling Excel what to do.

● Saving time and space

One of the main ideas behind adding the Task Pane options is to save time on commonly used commands, so freeing up more time for you to spend on actually working on your spreadsheets. Although each time you

use a Task Pane option, you may only save a click or two, over a few hours' computing it all adds up.

In addition, the Task Pane has much more space to display and explain its commands and options than is available through the toolbar or menu, so there's no need to try to remember the functions assigned to icons or keyboard shortcuts.

The default Task Pane is entitled New Workbook, and lists commands in much the same way as they are listed in the menus. However, the New Workbook Task Pane is just

one of several Task Panes, and the others utilize this space in a very different – and productive – way.

The Clipboard Task Pane lists the numbers, formulae and other items that you have recently cut or copied, making it easier to paste any of them into your spreadsheets. The Search Task Pane lets you search your computer for a specific document – all you need to know is some of the text it contains. Finally, the Insert Clip Art Task Pane displays small preview images to help you choose pictures to illustrate your worksheets.

PC TIPS

It is easy to switch the Task Pane on and off. If you open a new document to find that the Task Pane isn't visible, or you want to turn it off so that you have the maximum amount of space to work on your spreadsheets, simply click once on the View menu and then click on Task Pane.

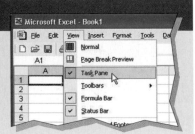

Choosing and using Task Panes

There are several Task Panes to choose from, and some use the extra space available to present powerful commands much more efficiently than the menu and toolbars.

1 The default Task Pane is called New Workbook, and provides a quick way of opening blank spreadsheets or switching to existing documents. For example, click on Blank Workbook in the New section and Excel opens a new blank spreadsheet.

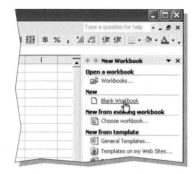

2 As you create and save your spreadsheets, the Open a workbook section grows, listing the spreadsheets you have most recently saved. You can click on any file listed here to open it. Excel knows where it stored the document, so you don't have to find it yourself.

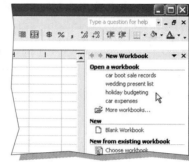

3 To switch to other Task Panes, click on the downward-pointing arrow just to the right of the New Workbook title. A short list drops down and you can now select the Clipboard.

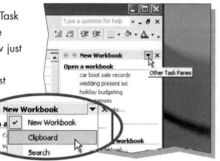

4 The Clipboard Task Pane appears; in this example it is blank because nothing has been copied or cut in the current Excel session. As you work on your spreadsheets, any material you copy or cut is listed in the main panel of the Task Pane (inset).

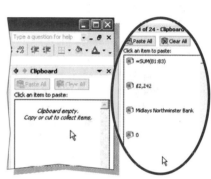

5 The benefit of this is that Excel's Clipboard is more powerful than Windows' own Clipboard, which can store only one item (see Stage 1, pages 16–17). This clipboard can store up to 24 items, and you can paste any of them whenever you like. Just click on an item in this Task Pane and it is automatically pasted into your spreadsheet.

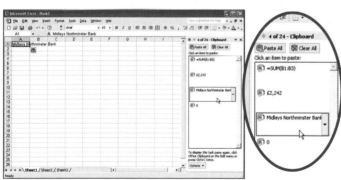

6 Select the Search Task Pane. This lets you find documents: simply type in a word or phrase and then click the Search button (inset).

7 Within a few moments, the Basic Search Task Pane lists matching files – click on one to open it.

8 As you use the different Task Panes, Excel keeps track of the order in which you use them. You can use the Back and Forward buttons (inset) next to the Task Pane title; they work just like the Back and Forward buttons in your Web browser.

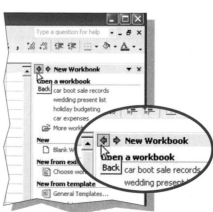

PC TIPS

If you prefer working with Excel's normal menu and toolbar commands, you can increase your worksheet area by telling Excel not to display the Task Pane every time it starts.

Untick the Show at startup box located at the bottom of the Task Pane.

Monitoring your mortgage

With its powerful calculation capabilities, Excel can help you make informed financial decisions. Here we look at how it can assist when you want to buy a home.

We've already seen how Excel can help give you a very clear idea of where your household budget is being spent (see Stage 1, pages 60-61). Excel can also be a great help when it comes to making important financial decisions. You can use Excel to simplify tricky calculations and compare costs, payments and interest rates at a glance.

By creating a worksheet in Excel, you can play with alternative scenarios – the kind of 'what if?' questions you have to ask yourself when making big decisions. If you're taking out a mortgage, for instance, you might ask yourself: 'Should I opt for the lender who offers the upfront discounts – or forget the discounts and go for the lender who offers slightly lower monthly payments instead?'

● How Excel rates

You can do this sort of exercise on the back of an envelope, with a pencil and a calculator, but it is messy and laborious and there is a high chance of getting your sums wrong. Also, to see the effect of small differences in the monthly payments between two loan offers, you have to work through the calculation by hand. By putting together some of the Excel features we have covered so far in *PCs made easy*, you can easily set up a spreadsheet that works out the overall costs automatically and enables you to see in an instant the effect of many different changes.

Opposite we have set up a worksheet that examines and compares two hypothetical mortgage offers. We don't delve into interest rates, but we do look at how other kinds of payments – survey, arrangement fee and so on – can affect the overall cost. In particular, we use Excel's number-crunching capabilities to help ensure that we see the full picture of the two finance deals that are on offer. We'll see how apparently massive savings in the upfront costs of one mortgage, for instance, might be wiped out in the long term by repayments of just a few pounds more.

By breaking a confusing range of costs down into simple, step-by-step calculations, Excel makes cost comparisons simple. Of course, you still have to check your sums – and take care to put the right figures in the right boxes. Excel does only what it is told.

You can use Excel to help with your calculations before signing on the dotted line, but always get someone to double-check your sums before making any long-term decisions based on the results.

Comparing mortgage costs

The great thing about Excel is that it lets you change individual parts of a calculation, showing you the effect each has on the other figures. Here we look at mortgage costs.

1 Start with a blank worksheet and add row headings as shown here. To make the calculations easier, we've divided our house-buying costs into one-off expenses (the arrangement fee and house survey) and monthly payments (insurance and repayments). Notice that the height of rows 7 and 13 has been reduced to bring the calculations closer: this is done in the same way as changing the width of a column (see Stage 1, pages 58–59).

2 Now we can start adding the figures from the first of the lenders. Add a column heading (we've used 'ABC bank') and then type in the figures. (Note: we've used some cell formatting to help make our worksheet easy to read – see Stage 1, pages 58–59 for details of how to add formatting to cells in your worksheet.)

3 For each of the subtotals, select the relevant cells (B6 and B11 in our example) and click on Excel's AutoSum button. Excel will add the two figures above each cell to produce the subtotals.

4 A simple formula will calculate the total of the repayments over the full term of the loan. Click on cell B12 and type '=B11*12*25'. This multiplies the monthly subtotal by 12 and then by the number of years (25 in our example). When you press the [Enter] key, Excel will calculate the figures for you.

PC TIPS

Quick copies

On page 55, we showed a quick way to copy cells. You can also use this technique to copy a formula. For example, delete the calculation from cell C6 and click on cell B6. Click on the small square at the bottom right of the cell and drag it one cell to the right. Release the mouse and you'll find that Excel not only copies the formula but automatically makes the appropriate adjustments to it in the process.

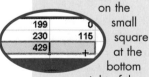

5 Now we'll add a formula to calculate the overall cost of the loan, including upfront costs and monthly repayments. In cell B14, type '=B6+B12' and press the [Enter] key.

6 Now we'll add some figures from another lender to see how they compare. In our example, this lender offers some special incentives: no loan arrangement fee and a half-price survey. Start by creating another column for the lender and add the initial figures as shown on the screen to the right.

7 Now add similar calculations for the subtotals, multiplications and additions for our second lender with higher repayments. Each formula will look almost identical to those used in steps 3, 4 and 5; but you must replace the 'B' in each formula with a 'C'. For example, in C14 you should type '=C6+C12' instead of '=B6+B12'. It's good practice to get used to entering such calculations by hand, but once you're confident with Excel formulae, you can use Excel's built-in intelligence. For example, if you use the Quick copies tip (left) for formula copying – where only the column or row name changes – you'll find these worksheets easier to make.

8 Finally, we can add a simple subtraction calculation to show the differences between the two loan quotations. Pick a cell (we've chosen D14), type '=C14-B14' and press the [Enter] key. Excel will now show the overall difference between the two loans as a single figure. From our hypothetical example, it's clear that despite the lower upfront costs of the quotation from XYZ bank, the loan is actually substantially more expensive in the long run. Use Excel for the number crunching, and you can focus on the real decision.

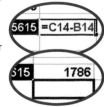

Calculating the effect of tax changes

Do you struggle with a calculator to work out how tax changes will affect you? Here's how to save trouble by setting up an Excel worksheet to do all the hard work for you.

In Stage 1 and on the previous two pages we have shown several examples of ways in which Excel can keep track of how you spend the money you earn. But what about the part of your salary that you never see: the money you pay in tax?

Whenever the government announces changes to tax rates or tax allowances in a budget, you will see people frantically tapping away at calculators, trying to work out how much better or worse off they'll be. However, you can make things a lot easier by setting up a simple Excel spreadsheet to do the number crunching for you. Once you have set up the basic headings, salary data and financial calculations, you need only type in the new details and let Excel work out automatically what the changes will mean for you.

● **Modifying your worksheet**

We'll see how you can do this using the Excel skills you've already learnt. In our example (opposite), we'll stick to a simple situation with just one change to the basic rate of tax and a straightforward tax-free allowance. Obviously, the way in which taxes are calculated varies from country to country and from one government to the next. You might also find that your tax situation changes when you get married. However, modifying

the worksheet to reflect these different situations is easy. Save the worksheet each time you make changes, and you'll be able to see the effect of promotions and pay rises – and new rates of tax – in seconds.

Don't let tax problems get on top of you. Instead of getting submerged in paperwork, try using your computer to tidy things up for you.

SIMPLIFY YOUR CALCULATIONS

The idea of setting up a spreadsheet formula to do your tax calculations might seem daunting. However, like so many practical problems, the task becomes much simpler if you break it down into smaller steps. So, instead of attempting to do the whole calculation using a single complicated formula, we've split it into three steps and set up an easy-to-understand formula for each one. The first formula calculates your taxable salary, the second one works out how much tax you have to pay and the final one tells you how much salary you'll have left after paying tax.

Step-by-step tax calculations

Tax is a complicated area, but the basic calculations are usually simple. We've used an easy example to show you how to break the calculation down into steps.

FIRST YOU need to set up some cells to type in the figures needed to perform the calculations: you'll need to set aside one cell for your annual salary, another for the tax-free allowance and the last for the tax rate. One way of handling the calculation is to create a formula in the next cell to work out your salary after tax in a single calculation. However, this formula would be complicated and it would be all too easy to make a mistake when typing it in. Instead, we'll opt for a step-by-step approach that uses separate formulae to calculate your taxable salary, the amount of tax payable and finally your salary after tax (see Simplify your calculations, opposite).

The other advantage of this technique is that it's easier to modify the worksheet to reflect changes and differences in the way that your tax is calculated.

PC TIPS

Monthly wages

You can also work out the difference that tax changes would make to your monthly wages by adding one more formula to the worksheet. To do this you need to calculate the difference between your salary after tax under the old tax rate and your salary after tax under the new rate; divide the result by 12 to get the monthly difference. Use the worksheet created in the steps opposite and click on cell D6. Type '=(C6-B6)/12' and press the [Enter] key. Excel now displays the difference as a monthly figure. In our example, it's a negative, indicating that we will be worse off with the new rate.

12000	
24	
2880	
12120	-20

1 We'll break the tax calculation down into simple steps with headings for 'Annual Salary', 'Tax-free Allowance', 'Taxable Salary', 'Tax Rate', 'Tax Payable' and 'Salary After Tax'. Type these into cells A1 through to A6.

	A
1	Annual Salary
2	Tax-free Allowance
3	Taxable Salary
4	Tax Rate
5	Tax Payable
6	Salary After Tax
7	
8	

2 The next step is to fill in the figures. Type your annual salary in cell B1, your tax-free allowance in B2 and type the percentage rate of tax in cell B4. In this example, the tax rate is 22 per cent, so we've typed in the number '22'.

B
15000
3000
22

3 Work out your taxable salary by subtracting your tax-free allowance from your annual salary: click on cell B3 and type '=B1-B2'. Press the [Enter] key and Excel will calculate the result.

	A	B	C
1	Annual Salary	15000	
2	Tax-free Allowance	3000	
3	Taxable Salary	=B1-B2	
4	Tax Rate	22	
5	Tax Payable		
6	Salary After Tax	3000	
7		12000	
8		22	

4 Next, let's calculate how much tax you have to pay. To do this we'll multiply your taxable salary by the tax rate and, because the rate is a percentage, divide by 100. Click on cell B5, type '=B3*B4/100' and press the [Enter] key. Excel will display the result instantly.

	A	B	C
1	Annual Salary	15000	3000
2	Tax-free Allowance	3000	12000
3	Taxable Salary	12000	22
4	Tax Rate	22	2640
5	Tax Payable	=B3*B4/100	
6	Salary After Tax		

5 The final step is to work out your salary after tax. This is simply your annual salary minus the tax payable. Click on B6, type '=B1-B5' and press the [Enter] key once more.

	A	B	C
1	Annual Salary	15000	
2	Tax-free Allowance	3000	
3	Taxable Salary	12000	
4	Tax Rate	22	
5	Tax Payable	2640	
6	Salary After Tax	=B1-B5	
7		12000	
8		22	
9		2640	
		12360	

6 Let's imagine the tax rate changes. To compare new and old salaries, we'll need a duplicate set of figures. We could type these – but it's better to get Excel to do the hard work. Use the mouse to highlight cells B1 to C6.

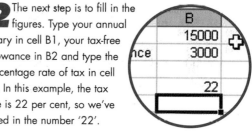

B	C
15000	
3000	
12000	
22	
2640	
12360	

7 Click the Edit menu and choose the Right option from the Fill sub-menu. Excel copies the contents of the highlighted cells in column B into those in column C.

8 Type the new rate of tax into cell C4 and press [Enter]. Excel will instantly work out the calculations in cells C3, C5 and C6. The C6 cell shows the overall effect of the new rate of tax.

	A	B	C	D	E
1	Annual Salary	15000	15000		
2	Tax-free Allowance	3000	3000		
3	Taxable Salary	12000	12000		
4	Tax Rate	22	24		
5	Tax Payable	2640	2880		
6	Salary After Tax	12360	12120		
7					
8					

Introducing CorelDRAW

In Stage 1, you learnt how to master Microsoft Paint. Now let's take a look at a more versatile graphics program – CorelDRAW. This section outlines what CorelDRAW can do and how to do it.

CORELDRAW VERSIONS

There are several different versions of CorelDRAW available. The best value package for home computer users is CorelDRAW Essentials, a cut-down version of the CorelDRAW Suite. CorelDRAW Essentials focuses on the two most useful Corel programs – CorelDRAW and Corel PHOTO-PAINT. It also includes plenty of clip art and sample photos to help you get started with computer graphics.

It costs around £70 instead of about £300 for the full Suite. The CorelDRAW Suite includes extra clip-art images and a number of extra programs. For example, CorelTRACE can convert scanned images into drawings which can be edited, and CorelTEXTURE allows you to create texture effects, such as marbling or textile finishes. In use, however, the two versions are almost identical, so you will be able to do the exercises in this course with either version.

Microsoft Paint is fine for simple projects and basic graphics, but for anything more polished and creative, you need a more versatile graphics program. One of the most popular art programs is CorelDRAW from the Corel Corporation.

● CorelDRAW advantages

The biggest difference between CorelDRAW and Paint is that CorelDRAW is vector-based, and Paint is bitmap-based. With Paint, you select an area of pixels (dots) and alter their colour. With CorelDRAW, you build a picture by plotting lines and points to draw objects (shapes). The advantage is that an object can be moved and remodelled with no effect on the rest of the picture. In Paint, you edit pictures by erasing or painting over areas. In CorelDRAW, you can change the colour or shape of any part of the picture. It's easy to use, too, using simple drag-and-drop techniques.

Making a start with CorelDRAW

Here are just some of the clever things that you can do with the power of CorelDRAW, using the same sort of Christmas card design as the one created in Stage 1, pages 80–81.

One of the good things about **objects** is that you can change their shape at any time. The Christmas tree in this example was difficult to draw in one go, so it was roughly sketched and then modified to the shape we needed. Any image can be altered in this way.

CorelDRAW comes with a range of clip-art images. As you can see from the dialog box below, you get a preview of each object to help you choose. In our Christmas card design, the snowflakes, clouds and the snowman's carrot nose are all clip-art objects.

You can build up pictures by drawing or importing simple shapes and then moving them together. You can overlap all these shapes exactly as you want and then choose whether to bring an object to the front or send it to the back. In our example, we can have the snowman in front of the Christmas tree – or behind it.

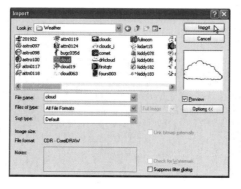

WHAT IT MEANS

OBJECTS

In vector-based drawing packages, each item in a picture is referred to as an object. This is because every line, shape, graphic and piece of text is separate from the others and can be edited and moved independently. This means you have a lot more scope to change and evolve your picture as you work on it – unlike a bitmap editing program such as Microsoft Paint. CorelDRAW can create and edit many different types of images, using options that just aren't possible in Microsoft Paint.

With CorelDRAW you can move objects separately or you can select groups of objects and move them together. Here we have selected all the objects that make up the snowman and moved them as a single item – tilting the snowman on its side (inset). We could do the same for the leaves and trunk of the tree.

CorelDRAW has a tool that lets you create any shape – by drawing it. Do this by defining the corners of an object (a little like you would with Paint's Polygon tool) and then you can turn any straight line into a jagged one. In our card, we've used a jagged edge to create an irregularly shaped mountain.

Any complete shape is an object and can be moved independently of every other shape in the picture. You could, for instance, pick up the snowman's head – without his face.

Alternatively, you can pick up and move a group of objects, such as the whole snowman. This lets you rearrange the image quickly or copy bits of one picture into another.

CorelDRAW gives all kinds of possibilities for texture and colour. There is a whole variety of textures on the clip-art CD-ROM, for example. By adding some of these colours and textures into a picture you can completely transform it, as we have done with our mountain.

CorelDRAW basics

Although the opening screen of CorelDRAW presents you with a mass of toolbars and buttons, it works in a similar way to the familiar Microsoft Paint or Word.

To start CorelDRAW, click on the Start button, select the All Programs option and then the CorelDRAW ESSENTIALS folder. Within this folder, you'll see a number of items that were installed along with the main CorelDRAW program. Select the option labelled CorelDRAW 9.

When the program starts up, you will see a Welcome to CorelDRAW window. This has several options: for now just click on the New Graphic icon. You will see the blank page screen shown below. Take a few moments to familiarize yourself with the major elements that are on this standard CorelDRAW screen.

The program window is very similar to most other Windows programs. If anything, with its two toolbars, toolbox and colour palette, it looks a little like a cross between Word and Paint. Many of the buttons are very similar to those of Paint. Some of the icons will look unfamiliar at first, but don't worry: we shall introduce them as we delve deeper into CorelDRAW. For our first step-by-step exercise, we'll get started by looking at CorelDRAW's basic shape-drawing features (opposite).

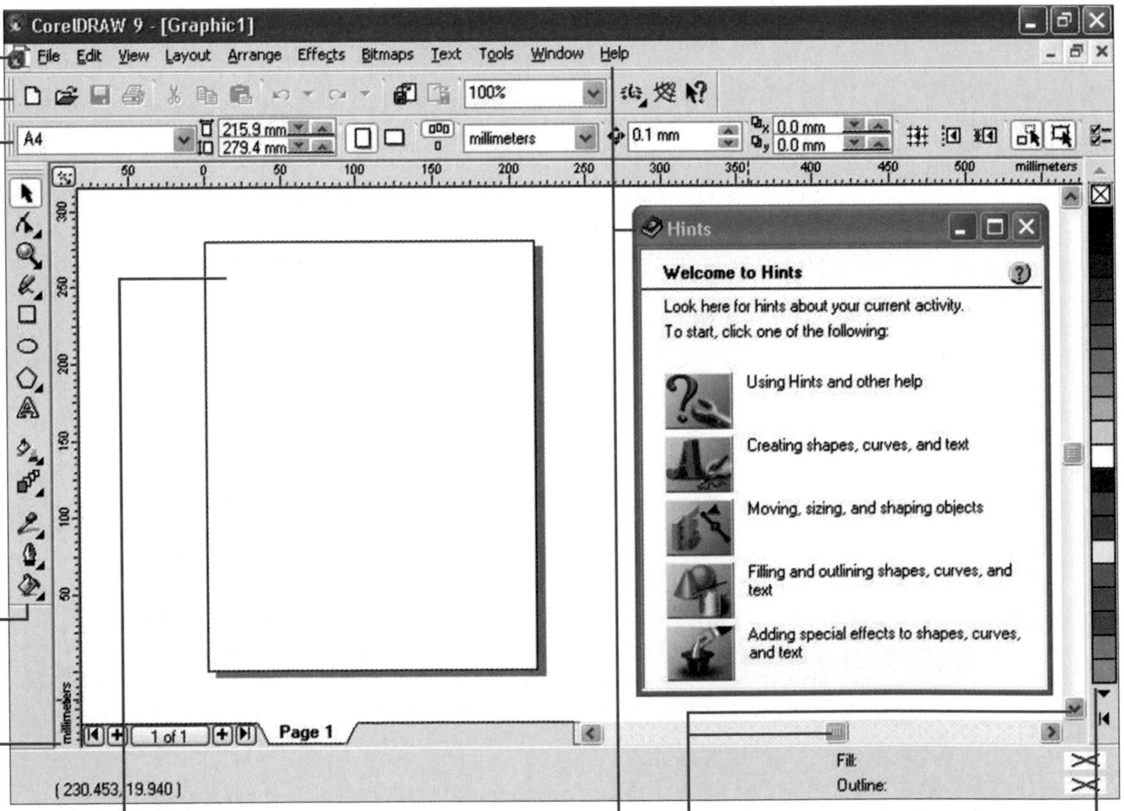

New Graphic

Menu bar
CorelDRAW's Menu bar gives you access to all the CorelDRAW commands.

Standard toolbar
On the first toolbar, you'll find buttons for frequently used commands such as opening and saving files.

Property bar
The second toolbar is used to change the properties – size, position and so on – of objects in your image.

Toolbox
The Toolbox contains the tools you will use most frequently when creating drawings and pictures.

Ruler
The ruler around the edge of the drawing area is in inches by default, but you can easily change this to a variety of other measures, including millimetres, as shown.

Drawing Page
This is the area where you draw your pictures. It is initially set as a US Letter sized page, but you can change it to any size, including A4, as shown.

Hints
Select Hints from the Help menu and another window floats on top of the CorelDRAW window, offering lots of useful hints for the first-time user.

Scroll bars
Like most Windows programs, CorelDRAW has vertical and horizontal scroll bars to let you move around the page.

Palette
You get a standard palette of colours by default, but it is possible to create and add your own colours to the palette.

Getting started with shapes

CorelDRAW's ability to let you move and colour shapes helps you to make effective pictures and graphics very easily from the simplest outlines. Here's how to get started.

PC TIPS

Object ordering

Things can get a little confusing using just the To Front and To Back commands (see Step 9), especially when you have multiple objects stacked on top of each other. You can move an object up or down one layer at a time by using the Order commands. Click on a shape with the right mouse button. You will see a pop-up menu: click on Order and select Forward One or Back One to move the object up or down in a stack of objects. In the example below, we have used the In Front Of command to move a green pentagon to the front of the stack, in front of the purple square.

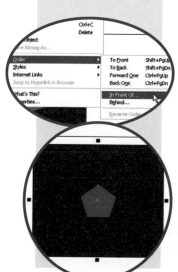

1 Let's start by drawing a few simple shapes. Look at the Toolbox located on the far left of your screen. Find the Rectangle Tool; it's the fifth tool from the top. Click on it once.

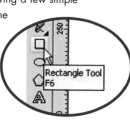

2 The Rectangle Tool works just like the one in Paint; click and hold the left mouse button where you'd like one corner of the rectangle and drag the mouse. You'll see an outline of the rectangle appear. Release the mouse button when the rectangle is the size you want.

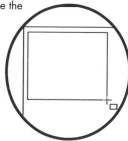

3 Now try an ellipse. Click on the Ellipse Tool, which is just beneath the Rectangle Tool on the Toolbox.

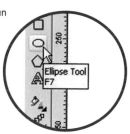

4 Again, the Ellipse Tool works just like the one in Paint. Click and drag from one corner of the ellipse to the other. Release the mouse button when you've got the shape you want. Don't worry if the ellipse isn't positioned exactly where you want it. You'll soon see how easy it is to move a shape around within your drawing.

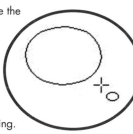

5 To change the colours of the two shapes you need to select each one in turn. Click on the Pick Tool at the top of the Toolbox and your cursor will change into a black arrow.

6 Now click on the rectangle to select it (eight small squares appear on its edges and an X appears in the centre). Fill it with colour by clicking on one of the colour squares in the colour palette on the right.

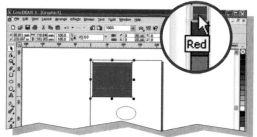

7 Select the ellipse you drew in Step 4. You can tell it is selected by the X in the centre of the object. Now choose a different colour for it.

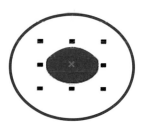

8 To illustrate the practical benefits of the way CorelDRAW works compared with bitmap-based programs, such as Microsoft Paint, we'll look at how to move and arrange these two simple shapes. Click on the ellipse with the left mouse button, and keep it pressed. Drag the ellipse so that it covers part of the rectangle. This action is very easy in CorelDRAW, but it's almost impossible with a bitmap program such as Paint.

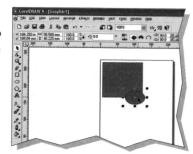

9 If you'd rather have the rectangle covering the ellipse, you can make it do just that with one click of the mouse. Select the rectangle and click the To Front button on the Property bar – the rectangle is now on top of the ellipse. Using these simple tools, you have the beginnings of a simple logo (bottom right) which might be used on a letterhead.

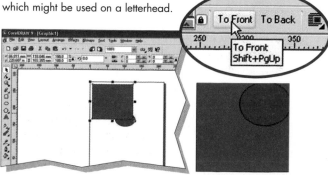

Making a poster

Creating attractive, eye-catching posters to advertise a local charity or artistic event – or simply to hang on your wall – couldn't be simpler with CorelDRAW.

CorelDRAW, with its ability to combine graphics and text, is perfect for creating posters. In CorelDRAW, you manipulate the component parts or objects of a picture. This lets you roughly sketch in the separate elements of your design, then work on them and move them around until you have the image exactly as you want it. The vast amount of clip art that comes with CorelDRAW is also a big help, as you'll find that it has at least a few images associated with most everyday items and activities.

The example we have used in this exercise is a poster for a Christmas bazaar. But you can, of course, equally well create lots of other designs, such as business cards, invitations, certificates and signs. Everything can be produced quickly and easily with the clip art and text options. The nature of CorelDRAW also means you can easily reuse parts of your design in other projects.

● **Graphic effects**

There is a wide range of easy-to-use effects that you can try with both text and pictures. You can rotate text or images to any angle, for example, with a single mouse movement. You can also use tools that allow you, with very little work, to add greater depth to your images and make text look more appealing. Simply adding

By using CorelDRAW, you can make many different styles and sizes of poster to suit your needs, whatever they happen to be.

a few extra colours to a scene here and there can also make it look much more interesting, attractive and eye-catching.

Once you start using CorelDRAW, you'll quickly pick up the basics and begin to try more advanced options, such as the **Perspective** Tool. These allow you to create some impressive results, with professional-looking images such as those shown on the following pages. It's no surprise that many professional graphic artists use CorelDRAW for just this type of work.

By mixing clip-art images and text effects, you can create anything from text illustrations to business cards.

Simple special effects – Rotation and Skew

In CorelDRAW, you can twist or turn pictures and words, making them any shape you want. This allows you to change them so that they fit into any space with just a few simple moves of your mouse.

THE KEY TO changing the shape of an object is the set of handles that appear on it when it is selected. These handles can be moved to make changes to your objects. At the simplest level, you can use the eight small black handles on the edges of an object to change its width and/or height. You do this in the same way as you would change an object's size in Word (see Stage 1, pages 48–49). CorelDRAW, however, has many more shape-changing options than Microsoft Word. Here we show you how to use two of the easiest but most useful: Rotation and Skew. With these you can turn objects about a central point, or make them appear slanted.

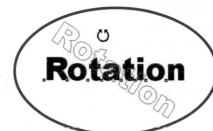
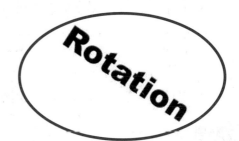

To use CorelDRAW's simple special effects, double-click on an object – we've selected a simple text object. You'll see a set of rotation and skew handles (above, left). Like the standard handles, there are eight of them positioned around the edge of the object and their appearance reflects their actions. There's also a dot inside a circle that represents the centre point,

which will be used for the actions you carry out on the object.

The rotation arrows appear at the four corners of the object and allow you to rotate it around the centre point. When you pick up one and drag it, you will see an outline of the object move to show the new position (above, centre). Release the mouse button and CorelDRAW redraws the object (above, right).

The skew handles are centred on the sides of the object and let you stretch it from side to side or from top to bottom (below, left). Drag the top centre handle to the right. As you drag it, a blue outline shows the object's new position (below, centre). When you release the mouse button, you'll see that the object is redrawn (below, right).

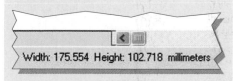

CAR FOR SALE

£2000 ono
TEL: 01459 4022394

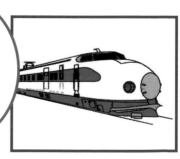

CorelDRAW's library of clip art covers a huge range of themes, with everything from motoring to events to trains. There's a good chance that there'll be something in the library for whatever type of poster you want to create. You can see what's in the library by browsing through the CorelDRAW manual. In it we found a section on Special Occasions, and in that was a folder full of Christmas tree images which, as you'll see on page 75, came in very useful.

Playing with text

With CorelDRAW, you can create some exciting poster effects just by moving and reshaping the text.

BEFORE YOU START working on your poster, write down all the information you can think of that needs to go on it – title, dates, times, prices and so on. As the first stage of your design process, it's a good idea to work out roughly where each piece of text needs to go. You can then begin by typing each part into a text box, as shown in the example below.

1 Click the Text Tool, marked A on the Toolbox (inset), and then click the mouse at the top of the page to start typing the first piece of text. Click on a new position to start each new text box until you have all your text items in roughly the correct position. Style your text as in Word (see Stage 1, pages 36–37).

2 You can move any text object as easily as moving a shape (see page 71). First, we'll rotate one of the text elements: select the Pick Tool from the Toolbox (inset) and double-click on the top line of text. This selects the particular part of the text you want to work with.

3 You will see the rotation and skew handles appear. Drag the bottom-right rotation arrow to the left with the mouse. Release the mouse to see the effect of your rotated text, then drag the text object up to the top right-hand corner of the page.

4 Another fun effect to try out is to add perspective to some of the text. This is a powerful tool that's very easy to use. Click on the Christmas Bazaar text (or whatever the most important text part of your poster is), then click on the Effects menu and select Add Perspective.

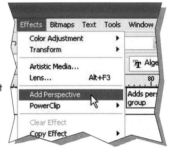

5 A red grid will appear over the text. At each corner are some small black handles. You can drag the handles to a new position and the shape of the text box will change: click on the handle at the bottom left corner of the grid and drag it downwards. As the outline shape of the object changes, you'll see the new shape of the letters in the text box.

6 Before we add the graphics (see opposite), we'll change the background colour from plain white. Click on the Layout menu and select Page Background from the list of commands.

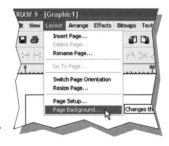

7 The Options dialog box appears. Select Solid, then select a colour from the drop-down palette.

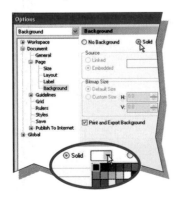

8 To give the poster more interest, we'll make the bottom half of the page a different colour. To do this, draw a rectangle over the bottom of the page. Colour it using the palette on the right of the window and then set it as the bottom layer (see page 71).

9 The rectangle has a black border, which is distracting. Change it to the same colour as the rectangle (green in our example) by double-clicking on the Outline box at the bottom right of the window. The Outline Pen window will appear; choose green from the drop-down list.

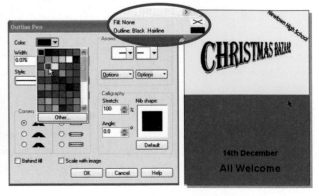

Playing with images

To make a really eye-catching poster, you can incorporate pictures from the CorelDRAW CD-ROM into your design. Here we show you how to start designing your own posters.

1 Insert the CorelDRAW clip-art CD-ROM into your CD drive and select Import from the File menu.

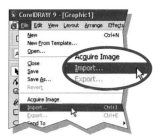

2 Use the Look in box of the Import dialog box to locate the Xmasanta folder. Double-click on the icon to see the folder contents.

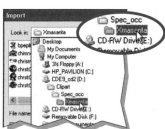

3 We have chosen 'chrst014.cdr', a picture of Father Christmas. Click once on its name and CorelDRAW will show you a preview of the file on the right side of the dialog box. (If the preview doesn't appear, tick the Preview box just above the Options button.) Click on the Import button.

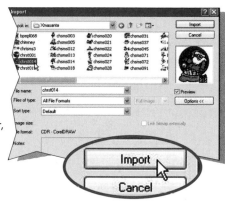

4 The mouse pointer changes to a corner icon. Click once to import the picture. When the picture is imported, it might be the wrong size. However, changing it is easy: drag one of the handles, just as you would do to change the size of a rectangle or an ellipse. First, click the padlock icon on the Property bar so that it is closed. This 'locks' the proportions of the picture so that any changes of size affect both height and width equally.

5 By moving one of the corner handles (below), you keep the same proportions. (Try unlocking the proportions and moving the side handles and CorelDRAW changes the proportions, right.) If you don't like the result, you can use the Undo button, or delete the selected image altogether and follow Steps 1–4 to start again.

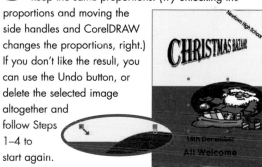

6 To round off the poster, we'll draw a circle around and behind the image. Select the Ellipse Tool from the Toolbox and draw a circle. Drawing a precise circle can be tricky, but by pressing the [Ctrl] key as you draw it, you will get a perfect circle every time.

7 You might need to move the circle slightly after you have drawn it. Use the Pick Tool to centre it around the image. You'll also notice that CorelDRAW has placed the circle on top of the picture. It would be better if the circle were behind it. To do this, click once on the clip art to select it, then click on the Arrange menu and select the To Front command from the Order menu.

8 Now our poster is complete. Using these simple text and clip-art techniques, you will be able to create many simple but effective posters. The only limitation is your imagination – so don't be afraid to experiment!

9 Don't forget to save your poster. CorelDRAW's save operations are much the same as those of Word and Excel. Use the Save in box to locate your *PCs made easy* or My Documents folder, type a name for your poster into the File name text box and click on the Save button.

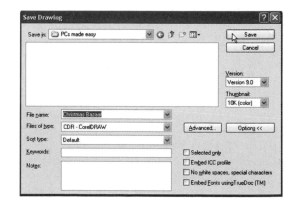

Working with curves

To get the most out of CorelDRAW you need to learn how to tweak its simple rectangle and ellipse forms into the exact shapes you need for your pictures. Convert the edges of a shape into curves and you can stretch it any way you want.

When using the standard Rectangle and Ellipse tools in CorelDRAW, you might have wondered how to create complex shapes. The answer is that rather than having a tool for every possible shape that you might want, you make a new shape by adapting a simple one to create something more complex.

As with most CorelDRAW drawing functions, the first step is to create a rough approximation of the desired shape and then gradually mould it into exactly the shape you need. Using and creating special curved lines is particularly important here, since most real-world objects contain curves, and computer images can look very false if they only contain straight edges, circles and ellipses. Fortunately, CorelDRAW is particularly adept at creating and manipulating curves.

● New tools, new shapes

CorelDRAW has just three standard shapes – rectangle, ellipse and pentagon. Even drawing quite simple objects such as an egg, a kite or an archway would be impossible without using CorelDRAW's curve tools.

To create new shapes, you start with a standard rectangle or ellipse and change the lines or curves used for its edges. You can take a shape with straight edges and convert any or all of its edges to curves.

By moving special handles on the edges of an object you can reshape it at will.

● Nodes and handles

In CorelDRAW, you can make complex shapes with nodes and bezier curves. For example, you can convert a rectangle with four corners into a rectangle with four nodes. Initially, the shape looks the same, but now you can drag each node into a new position to make new shapes. You can also add and delete nodes to change the shape further.

Most importantly, you can change the route taken by the line between nodes – this is very useful for creating shapes with smoothly curved edges.

Bezier curves are a little tricky to get the hang of initially, but with practice you will soon master them and be able to get far more impressive results than you could without them. Later in the course we'll show you how you can create bezier curves from scratch.

Turning shapes into curves

If you want unique and useful shapes in your drawings, you'll need to experiment with CorelDRAW's Shape Tool and bezier curves. Here's how.

THE POWER IN CorelDRAW lies in its ability to perform limitless changes to the shapes in your drawings. Even the simplest shape can be transformed into a more complex form that's almost impossible to create from scratch.

1 For this exercise, we'll show you how to transform an ordinary rectangle into a much more complicated curved shape. Start with a new, blank CorelDRAW page and select the Rectangle Tool from the Toolbox. Create a fairly large square shape on the blank page with the mouse.

2 Colour it with a bright colour by clicking on the colour palette (but leave the outline untouched for this exercise). To alter the shape of the rectangle select the Shape Tool from the Toolbox.

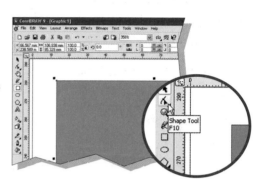

3 Now move the mouse pointer to one of the corners of the rectangle and click and hold the left mouse button. As you move the mouse up and down, and from side to side, you'll see a thin outline showing the rectangle gradually turning into a more circular shape.

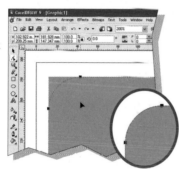

4 If you want to have greater control over the shape, and change it more radically, then you can convert it to a curved shape. There is a button on the far right of the Property bar called Convert To Curves. Click on this button to change the shape's edges into a sequence of curves.

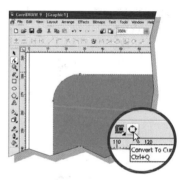

5 Now use the Shape Tool (see Step 2) again to move a node. You will find that you can move the node anywhere you want, not just within the restrictions of the original rectangle shape. You will also see extra lines and handles appear on the curves (inset).

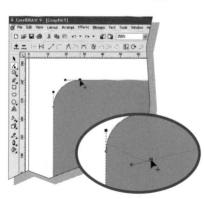

6 You will find that by altering the position of these handles in relation to the node they are attached to, you can make the curve steeper or shallower.

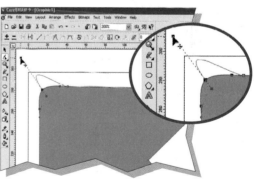

7 By adding new nodes (see right) to a simple shape, and by moving the control points of the nodes on your shape, you can create objects with a much more unusual shape than the one you started with. Your new shape is also unique which can add a more natural look to your images. Here we have copied and pasted a series of the same shape on top of each other, recoloured them and altered each one.

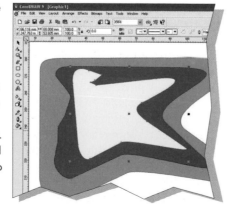

PC TIPS

Adding and deleting nodes

If you want more – or fewer – nodes in your shape, you can use the Add Node(s) and Delete Node(s) buttons on the Property bar. To delete a node, select it with the Shape Tool and click on the Delete Node(s) button. To add a node, select two adjacent nodes and click on the Add Node(s) button.

Using clip-art pictures

Even if you don't fancy yourself as much of an artist, you can still produce professional-looking pictures in CorelDRAW. This is thanks to a CD-ROM included with the program, which is full of ready-made clip-art images.

One secret to success in creating your very own high-quality images is to see how other such pictures are built up. CorelDRAW comes with a host of professionally created pictures – known as clip art – which you can copy, use wholesale or modify and adapt for your own artistic works. Most of the second CorelDRAW CD-ROM is packed full of these useful images – over 5,000 of them.

These pictures can be used in whatever way you want – either unmodified as they stand or as the basis for your own creations. If you are doing a simple document and want to add some interesting and colourful designs quickly, then you can easily import a clip-art image without ever needing to worry about drawing complex shapes.

● The clip-art advantage

If you look back to our first CorelDRAW picture of a Christmas scene (see page 69), you will remember that we used a clip-art image of a carrot for the snowman's nose. We could have drawn this, but the existing clip art was likely to be much better than our own hand-drawn image, unless we were to spend an inordinate amount of time on it.

You can also use clip art as the starting point for your own pictures. Imagine that you want to draw an aeroplane – a complex and time-consuming object to draw from scratch. It would be easier to import a clip-art image that is roughly what you want, then alter it to suit your exact needs. There is so much clip art stored on the CorelDRAW CD-ROM that you can be sure that for most subjects there

CorelDRAW comes with a host of professional images ready for you to use in your pictures. There are so many that there's a special catalogue of them included within the User Manual.

CorelDRAW ®

will be some sort of image associated with them. In fact, because there is so much it can take a long time to find the picture you want.

● Choosing a clip-art image

When you're using CorelDRAW itself, you can browse through the images by opening the Clipart window (under the Scrapbook entry in the Tools menu) and scrolling through the thumbnail pictures (small versions of the full pictures). But the easiest way to find what you want is to use the clip-art section of the CorelDRAW manual. This colour section of the book contains pictures of all the clip art stored on the CD-ROM. It also gives you the name of the folder and file where the clip art is stored.

CorelDRAW's clip art is split up into two main types of image – vector graphics and bitmap photos. The vector graphics include black-and-white and colour clip-art images, ready-made design templates for certificates and invites, and fonts. The clip art is stored on the second CD-ROM – as are the bitmap photos – and the templates and fonts are on the first CD-ROM. We'll deal with photos later in the course.

● Using clip art

We've already shown how to import clip art using the File menu (see page 75). This is the easiest method if you know which file you're looking for. If not, it is better to use the special Clipart window which shows how the folders on the CD-ROM are organized, together with previews of the clip art in each folder. To add the clip art to your picture, you simply drag and drop it from the window onto the page. Clip art often appears full screen, so the first thing you might have to do is shrink it to a more suitable size.

You can also alter and edit the clip art as if you'd created it yourself. A single clip-art image is made usually made up of lots of individual objects, just like any other CorelDRAW image. This means that you can change everything, from the colour of the smallest pane in a stained-glass window, to the number of figures in a crowd scene.

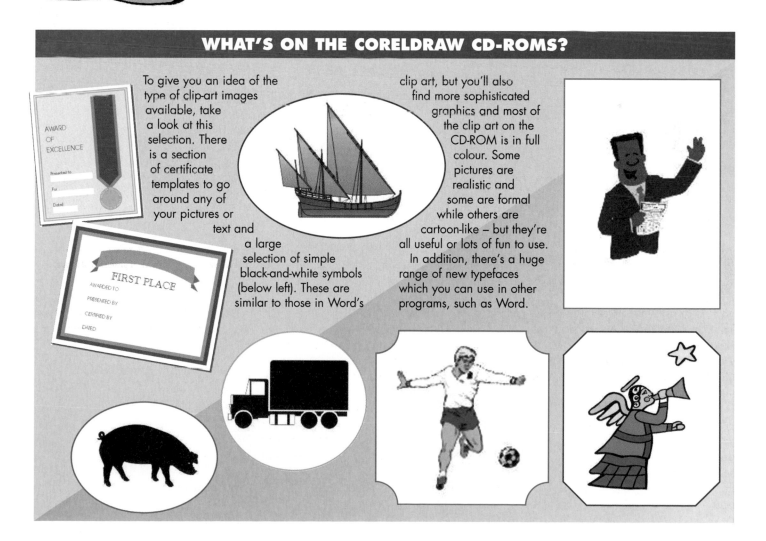

WHAT'S ON THE CORELDRAW CD-ROMS?

To give you an idea of the type of clip-art images available, take a look at this selection. There is a section of certificate templates to go around any of your pictures or text and a large selection of simple black-and-white symbols (below left). These are similar to those in Word's clip art, but you'll also find more sophisticated graphics and most of the clip art on the CD-ROM is in full colour. Some pictures are realistic and some are formal while others are cartoon-like – but they're all useful or lots of fun to use. In addition, there's a huge range of new typefaces which you can use in other programs, such as Word.

AWARD OF EXCELLENCE

Presented to

For

Dated

FIRST PLACE

AWARDED TO

PRESENTED BY

CERTIFIED BY

DATED

Working with ready-made clip art

Now you know how to import the clip art you want to use to make a picture, let's see just how much control you have over what the final image will look like.

1 You've already learned how to import clip art via the File menu, but you can also do it through a special dialog box. From the Tools menu, select Scrapbook and then click on the Clipart option.

2 A Clipart panel appears on the right of the CorelDRAW screen. Initially, it displays your Desktop icons. Put the second CorelDRAW CD-ROM into your CD-ROM drive and then select it from the list that appears when you click the downwards-pointing arrow at the top of the panel.

3 You won't see any pictures yet, as they are organized in folders. Double-click on the Clipart folder.

4 You'll see more folders, named according to the pictures in them. We want the 'eucar11' picture, which the manual tells us is in the Cars folder, within the Transpor folder. Double-click on each of these folders in turn.

5 The window will now display thumbnails of all the pictures in the folder. Use the scroll bars to look through the folder until you see the 'eucar11' file. Drag and drop it from the Clipart window onto the blank CorelDRAW page.

6 Once you have dropped in the picture, it appears on your page. It's made of many individual objects **grouped** together. We want to move individual parts of the picture. Click once on the picture to select it and then click the Ungroup button on the Property bar. Each element is indicated by a small square (inset, far right).

7 You'll now find that you can move the individual objects in the picture around on your page. Experiment for a while and you'll see just how this complex-looking picture is built up of numerous items.

8 With the objects ungrouped you can also change their colour properties. Right-click on the door, select Properties from the pop-up menu, click on the Outline tab, then click on the No Outlines button in the top right-hand corner. Click the Apply button to return to the picture and you'll see that the door no longer has a black outline.

9 You can change each element in any way you like. Clip-art images can also be used as the basis for your own pictures, so you don't have to start from scratch every time. Try selecting the white number plate and changing its colour by clicking on yellow in the palette; then you can paint the car zany colours by selecting and colouring separate parts of it in the same way.

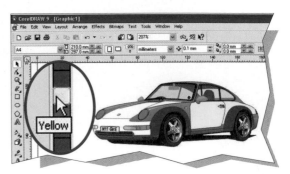

Using clip art in your own pictures

Clip art is often extremely useful as a basis for creating your own pictures and it's generally easier than starting from scratch. Let's see how this works by practising with some dining images to make a piece of artwork to use as a logo for a café.

1 Start with a piece of clip art of kitchen utensils from the Clipart folder under Home, then Kitchen. Let's change the colour of the utensils' handles. First click on the whole image and ungroup all the elements so we can work with them. We could select each individual utensil handle, but we'll use CorelDRAW's grouping facility instead. Hold down the left mouse button and draw a rectangle around all three handles. When you release the mouse button, you will see that all the objects within the rectangle are selected.

2 We don't want to colour the holes in the handles, so press and hold the [Shift] key and click once on each hole in turn. The small squares for the holes disappear. Now release the [Shift] key. Then click on the Group button on the Toolbar to join the three untensils' handles into a single object.

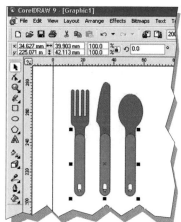

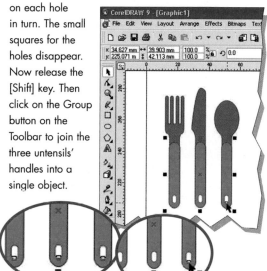

3 Use the left and right mouse buttons to select both fill and outline colours from the palette to colour the handles.

4 We are going to add the image of a dinner serving to our picture, so we need to reposition the cutlery around a space. Ungroup the individual utensils by clicking on the Ungroup button. Then click on the Pick Tool and drag each utensil into place. Rotate the spoon into position (see page 73).

5 Now we will import our new picture from the same folder, entitled meals065. Either drag it from the Clipart window as before (see page 80), or import it from the File menu (below).

6 Re-position your items by selecting each in turn with the Pick Tool and dragging them until you are happy with the arrangement.

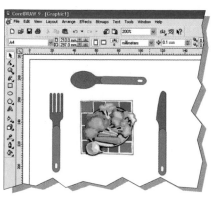

7 If you find that you no longer need an element of the picture, for example the spoon, click the item you want to delete and either press the [Delete] key on the keyboard, or select delete from the Edit menu. To select several parts of the picture, hold the [Shift] key down while you select them all.

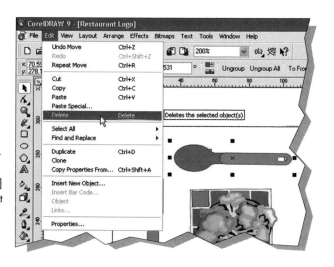

Using CorelDRAW's wide range of patterned and textured fills, you can create dozens of different effects as if by magic!

Special colour tricks

If you want to add subtlety and texture to your pictures, CorelDRAW's extensive range of fill options are just the thing.

So far, our CorelDRAW pictures have ended up looking a little gaudy and unrefined. This is in large part due to the solid and uniform fill that CorelDRAW uses by default. With only a single, flat colour for the shape, this can look unnatural and cartoon-like. But there are many other fill effects you can use to make your pictures look more exciting and realistic.

● Different types of fill

There are six basic types of fill. The No Fill option is a type of fill that is actually more useful than it sounds, as it means you can wipe an object clean of any pattern or colour and start from scratch with it. Uniform Fill is the standard type and is the most similar to the fills in Microsoft Paint; it simply fills in an object with a solid colour.

More interesting is Fountain Fill, as it allows for a blend of colours within the object. It also lets you choose the way the colours blend together. Pattern Fill, as the name suggests, fills an object with repeating patterns, such as a chequerboard of black and white squares. Texture Fill is similar to Pattern Fill, except it uses complex patterns created by fractals. Textures are excellent for realistic fills because they look less repetitive than patterned fills.

The final type of fill is PostScript Fill. This is mainly aimed at professional graphics users who use special PostScript printers for very high-quality printing. Home computer users won't need to use PostScript Fill.

● Experimenting with fills

As with many programs, it's well worth experimenting with these fill options. As you become familiar with them, you will find that by choosing the right fill you can quickly create drawings that would otherwise require a lot of effort. In the exercise opposite, we'll use both Fountain and Texture fills to colour in some simple objects. With a few clicks you can transform even the simplest of drawings into a much more realistic image with surprisingly subtle fill effects.

Using shades and textures

You're not limited to cartoon-like solid fills with CorelDRAW. Many of the best-looking pictures use shaded and textured fills to create realistic and attractive graphics. Here's how even the simplest of drawings can benefit.

1 Start by drawing a simple picture. Here, we've created an Easter chick from a few very simple shapes.

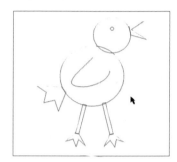

2 We'll start by colouring the chick's body. We could use a solid yellow, but a more subtly shaded fill would look better. First, select the body, click on the Fill Tool at the bottom of the Toolbox and then select Fountain Fill Dialog from the extra buttons that pop out.

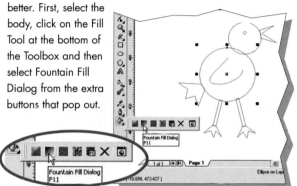

3 The Fountain Fill dialog box appears; click on the Type drop-down list at the top left and change it from Linear to Radial.

4 The small preview at the top right will change from its original, horizontally shaded square to show the Radial (circular shaded) fill.

5 The preview is shown in black and white, but you can tell CorelDRAW which two colours to use for the fill. For our chick we'll choose two shades of yellow. In the Color blend section, click on the From button. You will see a drop-down panel of colours. Scroll down until you find a suitable colour and then click on it. Choose another colour for the To button in the same way.

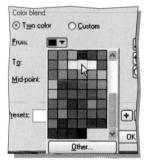

6 You'll see that the square preview of the fill at the top right changes to show your new colours. If it doesn't look right, go back and change the colours. When you're happy, click on the OK button and the fill will be applied to the chick's body.

7 You can repeat the process with similar colours on the head and tail feathers, but right now we'll try a textured fill. Select one of the legs and click on the Texture Fill Dialog button.

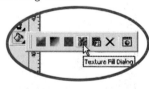

SHORT CUTS

When creating pictures, you'll often find that you use the same objects again and again.

CorelDRAW lets you duplicate an object or a group of objects. First select the item and press [Ctrl]+[D]. A copy will appear next to the original. This is quicker than using Copy and Paste commands.

8 CorelDRAW has plenty of ready-made textures to use in your pictures. The Texture Fill dialog box shows previews of the textures and allows you to customize them. Select Samples 7 from the Texture library drop-down box, scroll down the list of textures and select Wool.

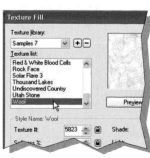

9 We want the texture to use colours appropriate for the chick's legs. Use the Shade and Light buttons on the right of the Texture Fill dialog box to select new colours. Also, change the Softness scale to around 75%, so that the pattern stands out more.

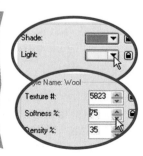

10 Use the same techniques to colour in the rest of the picture. Try out some of the other textures. Many are useful for different types of pictures, such as clouds and building materials.

WARNING DIALOG BOXES

When you change colours in the Texture Fill Dialog box (see Step 9), CorelDRAW warns you that it will convert colours to an RGB model (we'll explain this later in the course). This is fine, so you can click the OK button to proceed. You might want to tick the Don't show warning again box to avoid such warnings in the future.

Simple special effects

The computer-generated artwork that you see in magazines might look dauntingly complex, but many of the special effects employed can be accomplished with very little effort using CorelDRAW.

CorelDRAW's special effects usually work by altering or distorting an object you already have in your drawing. With the subtlety they add, you can create an impressive range of graphic images, some of which would not disgrace a professional designer.

The special effects are all available from the Effects menu and a few even have their own icon in the CorelDRAW Toolbox. Most are simple to add and will operate automatically, so you don't need to be a graphics expert to give your drawings a special sparkle.

● Experiment with effects
In the following pages, we'll look at some of the most useful effects. You'll see how to: blend two objects together; simulate the view through special camera lenses; make a two-dimensional object look three-dimensional; and make an object appear transparent.

● Flexible drawing tools
Special effects are flexible tools that can be edited when you apply them, or later, to change the effect they have on an object. Although effects alter the appearance of an existing object, the underlying object remains in the picture and can itself be edited at any time after the effect is applied.

The only exception is that objects which have already had one complex effect applied to them cannot then be modified by another. For example, you can't blend two objects together and then make them transparent.

When using CorelDRAW special effects, the only limitation to what you can achieve is your own imagination.

Otherwise, you can experiment as you wish: copy effects between objects or 'freeze' the effect and then copy and move that as a separate object of its own.

It is important not to use too many effects in a single picture or they will seem intrusive and gimmicky. But used in moderation, they can turn a simple image into an impressive one. The difference is a matter of 'taste' – something your PC can't provide. This is what makes computer art just as creative as any other form of visual expression.

The four main special effects

Here we look at four of CorelDRAW's most useful and versatile effects. They are all easy to use and give impressive results very quickly.

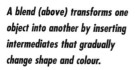

● Applying a blend

Blending is one of the most versatile special effects and can be applied to any objects you create using CorelDRAW. When you blend two objects, the program automatically creates a progression of intermediate shapes that gradually transform from one object into the other.

A blend (above) transforms one object into another by inserting intermediates that gradually change shape and colour.

You can still edit and move the original two objects (as well as the entire blended object), but not the intermediates. The line along which the blend occurs can be straight or curved and you can alter the number of steps. With a lot of steps, the end result is an elongated shape showing a smooth transition between the two original objects. You can also create a compound blend so that the effect works between more than two objects.

Lenses can turn simple shapes and colours into attractive patterns. The circle below is acting like a 'rose-tinted filter' on top of the hexagons.

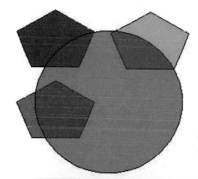

● Lens effects

CorelDRAW offers numerous lens effects that allow you to simulate the use of certain types of camera lens on your picture. Just like the real thing, the lenses in CorelDRAW change the appearance of objects viewed through them. The type of change produced depends on the shape of the object and the type of lens chosen.

In our example on page 86, we will be using a fish-eye lens, but there are lots of other lens effects you can try out, such as magnify, brighten and tinted greyscale.

● Extruding an object

When you extrude an object, you extend it backwards or forwards to give it the illusion of depth. In creating this effect, CorelDRAW adds extra surfaces to give an object a three-dimensional appearance. This can be a very

Extrusion makes a two-dimensional shape look three-dimensional. In this example, the word 'Success' is extended backwards, and enlarged during the process, creating a dramatic appearance.

effective way to create complex shapes without having to draw them. For example, extruding a rectangle can create a box shape, while extruding a circle can create a cylinder.

You can have lots of fun with this effect. Extrusion works with more complex shapes, as well, and you can even apply it to text.

● Transparency effects

You can set a transparency level through the Effects menu or through the Interactive Transparency Tool. Both let you control the colours, patterns and textures displayed to create very subtle shading.

OTHER SPECIAL EFFECTS

Add Perspective

This gives extra depth to a drawing by distorting objects to make them look as though they are disappearing into the distance.

Envelope

Envelopes enclose an object in an Imaginary 'stretchy frame' which can then be reshaped and distorted. They work particularly well with text.

PowerClip

This command allows you to put one object inside another object. Any changes made to the 'container' will then have the same effect on the object inside.

Contour

Applying contours creates an effect similar to the colours used to show height on a map. This works well on drawn shapes and also on text.

Here, transparency effects have been used to create a subtle, graduated colour on the 'sun' behind the flying bird.

Using CorelDRAW's blend effect

Here we illustrate how blending works on two simple shapes. The Interactive Blend Tool is powerful and versatile, with settings that can be altered to create more subtle effects.

1 To show the basic principles of blending, create two simple shapes a short distance away from one another and fill them with different colours, as we have done here (see pages 70–71).

2 Click on the Interactive Blend Tool in the Toolbox.

3 Click on one object and drag the mouse cursor on to the second. The direction determines which object ends up 'in front'.

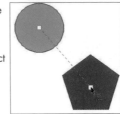

4 Release the mouse button and CorelDRAW will create a series of intermediate shapes in a straight line from the first object to the second. You can still edit the original objects to create further effects. Select the red pentagon and move it around. As you do so, you'll see the blend move to follow the shape (right).

5 You can achieve more subtle effects by editing the end objects. Use the Rotation box (inset) to turn the red pentagon. When you release the mouse, you will see the pentagon change to reflect its new orientation, together with all the intermediate shapes in the blend.

Lens effects

These effects make an object behave like a camera lens. There are several different lens options, but they all work in a similar manner.

1 To begin, create four simple filled shapes. Make sure the objects are quite close to each other, as in this example, to ensure that the effect of the lens is obvious. Select one of the objects to be your 'lens'.

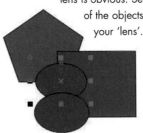

2 Click on the Effects menu and select the Lens command from the drop-down menu.

3 The Lens window appears. Select the Fish Eye option from the drop-down menu, then press the Apply button. The object selected becomes transparent because it has become your lens. Here you can see the subtle fish-eye distortion on the edge of the blue and red shapes (inset, right). The green shape is unaffected because it is in front of the lens.

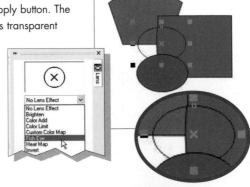

4 By default, the lens is pointing at the centre of the object. To move the viewpoint of the lens, tick the Viewpoint box in the Lens window, then click the Edit button.

5 You can move the lens viewpoint wherever you like (when you are changing the viewpoint, it is indicated by the larger cross), then press Apply in the Lens window to see the change (right). Experiment with moving the viewpoint and seeing how it affects your picture.

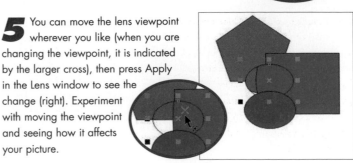

How to extrude an object

Extrusion is a great effect to use on text and simple pictures, giving them depth and dimension.

1 Start by creating a simple shape, using bezier curves or one of the ready-made shapes from the Toolbox.

2 Now click on the small arrowhead on the fourth button from the bottom of the CorelDRAW Toolbox then select the Interactive Extrude Tool from the set of tools that appears.

3 Click on your shape and drag the mouse in the direction you want the extrusion to appear. A wireframe outline shows the thickness of your extrusion.

4 The extruded sides of your shape have the same colour as its front. To make the 3D effect more obvious, click on the Property bar's Lighting button (inset) and click on 1.

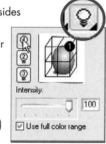

Intensity
100
☑ Use full color range

5 This casts some light and shade on to the object. The sides are now easier to see.

6 There's a small white marker on the extrusion line that is shown on your shape. Drag it back and forth to vary the depth of the extrusion.

Using the transparency effect

The main use of the Interactive Transparency Tool is to apply subtle shades, instead of solid blocks of colour, by letting you mask out part of the original colour.

1 To try some simple transparency effects, create a drawing with several different coloured circles on top of one another. Then click on Select All, then Objects in the Edit menu.

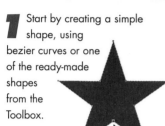

2 Click on the small arrowhead on the fourth button from the bottom of the CorelDRAW Toolbox and select Interactive Transparency Tool from the Toolbox.

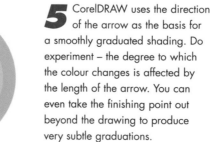

3 Go to the Property bar and select Uniform from the drop-down menu shown. Ensure that the slider that appears to its right is at the midway point. This creates a 50 per cent solid colour transparency, so 50 per cent of the original colour shows through. This has the effect of softening the colours in the drawing (right).

4 Transparency effects don't have to be solid or uniform. With the Interactive Transparency Tool still selected, click once to create a starting point for the transparency effect and hold down the button. An arrow appears. If you move the mouse, the arrow will follow the pointer. Drag it across the drawing and release it to indicate a finishing point for the effect.

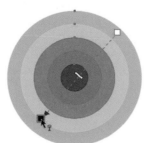

5 CorelDRAW uses the direction of the arrow as the basis for a smoothly graduated shading. Do experiment – the degree to which the colour changes is affected by the length of the arrow. You can even take the finishing point out beyond the drawing to produce very subtle graduations.

CorelDRAW ®

Combining objects

We've already seen how grouping objects together can help us move a composite image to a new position (see pages 80–81). Here we see how combining objects can make our creative drawing both easier and quicker.

Creating even a simple illustration in CorelDRAW involves bringing together a number of different objects. (The primitive snowman we drew in the exercise on page 69 involved a dozen or so items and even a simple piece of clip art can involve many more than that.)

Controlling all these different objects can be a fiddly business, but we have already looked at how you can group objects so that you can move them all together in one go.

However, on some occasions you'll find it more flexible, practical and efficient to combine the separate elements instead.

● Group differences

The Combine command converts all selected objects into a single, curved object – automatically creating nodes you can edit – with uniform fill and outline characteristics. This is different to grouping, which still treats each object as separate and distinct, even though you can move them around together.

If any of the combined objects overlap, CorelDRAW creates 'clipping holes', allowing you to reveal what's underneath and making it easier to get at the node of an object that's sitting behind another.

As well as allowing you to create complex shapes, combining objects dramatically reduces the file size and the amount of time it takes to redraw the screen. It's far smoother to move around a complex arrangement of combined objects than a stack of grouped

objects, each one of which has to be individually drawn by the computer.

It's easy to combine and then break apart objects. For example, in a complex creation you might find it easier to combine a number of elements and then work on them as a simple line drawing. To add colour you simply break them apart (see PC Tips, opposite).

● Combining text

Just as objects can be combined, the same principles can be used effectively with text. When you use the Combine command with text, the letters behave just like any other object that has been combined, and they become outlined shapes. When you move the combined text over other items, these show through (see PC Tips, right). Using Combine is the easiest way to achieve this effect.

PC TIPS

If you combine some text with a coloured rectangle to create a banner heading, you can then overlay the combination on top of a picture (right). The picture will show through the text to create an interesting effect.

Success

Making a picture frame

Picture frames don't necessarily have to be rectangular. By combining two objects, one inside the other, you can create any number of interesting alternatives.

THERE ARE MANY reasons why you might want to combine objects. To see how useful combining is, we will create an interesting-looking picture frame and then place an image inside it.

For the image in our example below, we have used a CorelDRAW photo ('625014' in the Photos-Places-England folders of the second CD-ROM). You can, of course, use any image that you wish for this example.

1 First create a circle and fill it in with a colour. Make sure the circle takes up most of the page. Remember that you can create a perfect circle (instead of an ellipse) by pressing [Ctrl] as you draw.

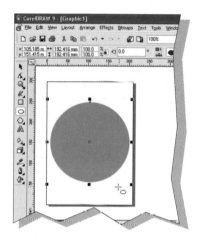

2 Next, create a pentagon shape in the middle of the circle with the polygon tool. Once again, you can make sure all its sides are even by pressing [Ctrl] as you draw it. To illustrate how Combine works, fill in the polygon in a different colour, even though its shape will soon become a clipping hole.

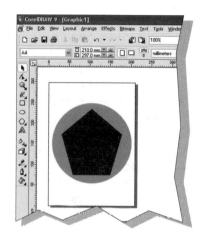

3 With the two shapes drawn, select them both with the Pick Tool. You'll notice that when you do so, the Property bar will automatically display the Combine button (if it's not there already). Click on Combine and watch as the two shapes combine. The area of overlap (the whole of the polygon shape) will become a clipping hole.

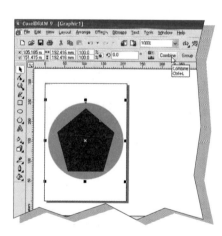

4 Even though the two shapes have been combined, you'll find that, thanks to the clipping hole, you can still edit the nodes of the original polygon object. Try this out with the Shape Tool and see if you can change the pentagon into a star shape, as we have done here.

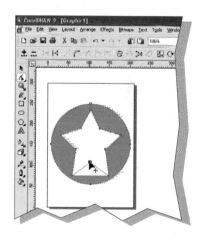

5 Now load in your image (see page 75). To see how the clipping hole allows other objects to appear through it, simply send the clip art to the back of the page. We've also adjusted the shape of the clip art by dragging the edges in using the handles, so that it doesn't poke out from the side of the circle.

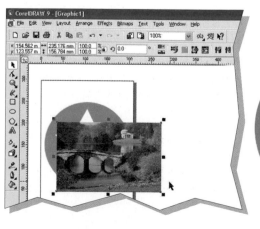

PC TIPS

You can un-combine objects just as easily as combining them. Select a combined object and then select Break Apart from the Arrange menu. This will divide the combined object into its original parts.

Hardware

Sound advice

Your computer has great noise-making potential, from simply playing a compact disc to recording a song. Here's how to wire your PC for sound.

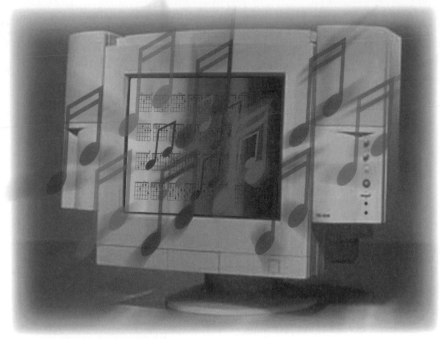

Computers can record and play back sounds and music to the same high quality used on audio compact discs. You can use your PC to help you compose and write music and link it to computer-compatible musical instruments. Then you can create any sound you like – from a rock band to a full orchestra.

If you only want to listen to music while you work at your computer, you can use it to play your favourite audio CDs or MP3 files from the Internet.

Check the rear of your PC to see if it has an output for headphones. If it does, you can use ordinary personal stereo headphones, which will make your game-playing and music-making more tolerable for others.

Your PC can even program the order in which it plays each track on a normal music CD, just like any top-of-the-range compact disc player.

Sound and music are also very important in most computer games and your PC can produce stunning sounds and effects, in stereo and surround sound, that will enhance any game you play. It is likely that

Plug your PC into your hi-fi system if you don't want the expense of buying speakers. You'll still hear good quality sound.

Budget PC speakers can produce good enough sound for occasional game play and music, but if you're serious about music, you should consider upgrading – perhaps installing a sub-woofer to add bass.

your computer is already capable of making all the noise you want it to. Have a look through the manuals that came with it to discover its noise potential. Refer to the guide opposite to find out what all the various music sockets on a typical computer are for.

● Sounding good

The quality of the sound that you hear will depend a lot on the quality and type of loudspeaker that you connect to your computer. If you aren't happy with the sound of your current speakers, it may be possible to improve them, either by replacing them or adding a sub-woofer.

If you have a hi-fi, there's a cheaper

Many multimedia PCs come with stereo speakers to enhance the learning and entertainment experience. If your PC doesn't have speakers, they can be added.

way of improving your computer's sound output. If your hi-fi is near your computer, you can use this to play the music and sounds from your PC. You will have to buy a cable to connect the sound card (see Stage 1, page 93) to the Line-in socket on your hi-fi amplifier.

A microphone can provide a link between your voice and the PC. By passing on the sound signal to speech recognition software, your PC can interpret your voice, allowing you to dictate documents instead of typing, for example.

WHAT IT MEANS

SUB-WOOFER

The loudspeakers that are used with computers are usually rather small. This means that they are not always good at producing deep bass musical notes. For bass notes, you need a larger speaker or a special device called a sub-woofer. A sub-woofer works with your normal speakers and makes sure that the deep, low bass sounds are played properly. Although adding sub-woofers will improve the sound from your computer, they can be quite expensive.

A look at the sockets for sound

Just like the rear of a hi-fi system, your PC has an array of sockets into which you can plug your musical accessories. Here's your guide to the sound sockets you'll find on a typical PC and what they do.

MIDI port

Although the icon indicates this is the joystick port, it can also be used to link your computer to an electronic musical instrument that can be controlled using signals called MIDI codes (MIDI stands for Musical Instrument Digital Interface). You can connect a MIDI synthesizer, drum machine or keyboard to your PC and input signals to the computer's sound card.

Audio output socket

To hear sound and music, you need to connect speakers to the sound card. The music from compact discs (and many games) is in stereo, so you will need two loudspeakers. Computer speakers are all fitted with the same small jack plug – push it into the socket indicated on the back of your computer. Depending on the type of loudspeakers you choose, you might need to plug them into the mains as well as your PC.

Headphone socket

Some PCs have a separate headphone socket that lets you plug a pair of standard personal stereo headphones into the sound card to listen to music or game sounds. If your PC doesn't have a headphone socket, try plugging some personal-stereo headphones into the audio output socket.

Microphone socket

If you want to record your voice or other sounds, you will need to plug a microphone into the sound card. Many Multimedia PCs are supplied with a microphone, or you can buy one from an electrical retailer.

Line-in/Aux-in

This socket is used when you want to record sound from your hi-fi. Some computers need an adaptor for this purpose. Only one socket is shown here – your PC might have two that match the two phono outputs on your hi-fi. Check your computer's manual for details.

Line-out/Aux-out

A few PCs have an extra socket that lets you play sound from your computer through your hi-fi's speakers. Connect the Line-out/Aux-out to a spare input on your hi-fi to play sounds through your hi-fi. If your PC lacks such a socket, you can get perfectly good results by using the audio output socket instead.

❶ **The parallel port**
Some older printers use this port.

❹ **The USB (Universal Serial Bus)**
This is standard for adding extra devices.

❷ **The monitor socket**
Your monitor is plugged in here.

❺ **The PS/2 mouse port**
This is a specially designed socket for the mouse.

❸ **The serial port**
Used for a mouse or external modem.

❻ **The keyboard socket**
Looks the same as the six-pin mouse socket.

Advanced printing

Your printer can do so much more than produce formal letters. Even a basic printer can handle many paper shapes and sizes, allowing you to create all kinds of fun documents.

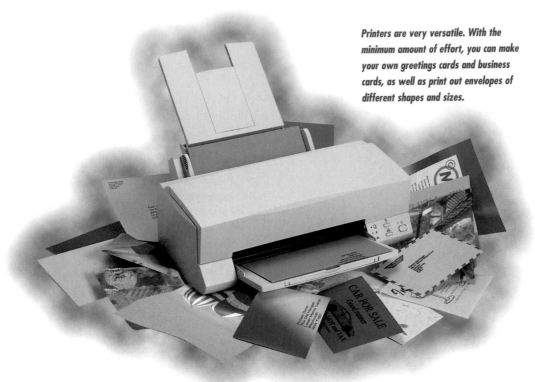

Printers are very versatile. With the minimum amount of effort, you can make your own greetings cards and business cards, as well as print out envelopes of different shapes and sizes.

A printer is one of the most useful accessories you can buy for your computer, and the range now available includes many flexible and powerful machines. If you've only used your printer for letters, you've missed out on features that can turn it into a home print shop. For example, you can change the direction in which you print from portrait to landscape format, which is ideal for wide tables, photographs or text (see Portrait And Landscape, right).

● Paper types

The usual way of working with a printer is to fill it with standard paper and print out letters. However, your printer can work with a variety of different paper types, including thicker writing paper, index cards and even business cards. You can change from the normal A4 size of paper and print on small sheets for your diary or personal organizer.

The printer isn't limited to sheets of paper – you can print an address directly onto an envelope or even print onto transparent plastic for presentations. If you want to send a letter to several friends or contacts, you can print their addresses onto a sheet of peel-off labels.

Your printer can help you keep your computer area organized more effectively: there are sheets of special labels that you can use to print labels for floppy disks or CD-ROMs. All you have to do is type the details into your PC (where you can store these details) and then follow a few on-screen instructions before you press the Print button.

● Special features

Many of your printer's special features are set up either from Windows or from a word processing program such as Word – you do not have to learn how to program your printer. This means that you can change the way you print in a few mouse clicks – and without even altering the settings of your printer.

It's easy to see where the portrait (above) and landscape (right) formats get their names from when you see them together.

PORTRAIT AND LANDSCAPE

The usual way of creating a letter or document is to write or print on a sheet of paper with the longest sides running downwards. This is known as portrait format, because portrait painters have always traditionally painted this way (you are reading this page in portrait format). Turn the paper on its side, and this is called landscape format, because this is the most suitable format for a panoramic landscape painting.

Great ways to get more from your printer

Your printer is capable of providing a lot more than just simple letters. Here we show you how to put power into your printing.

Almost every printer allows you to print a document either in portrait or landscape format. Portrait is the usual way of printing a letter, but landscape can be useful if you want to print wide spreadsheets, a sign or a banner. The paper always travels through your printer in the same direction, so to print in landscape format the printer turns the text or image sideways.

● Print a For Sale sign
Let's use the landscape format to print a For Sale sign for a car. Using Word, type in a few words suitable for a sign (below) and vary the size of

the text for legibility and impact (see Stage 1, pages 36–37). You might also want to centre the text on the page and insert a car graphic using clip art (see Stage 1, pages 46–49). Next, from the File menu, choose

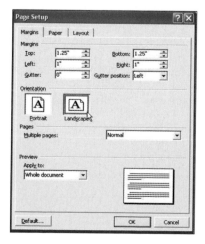

Page Setup and then select the Margins tab (bottom, left). You'll see a choice for paper orientation – choose Landscape (see how the Preview image at the bottom changes) and then click on OK to save this change. Finally, click on Print as normal. There is no need to make any changes to the printer itself.

● Printing on both sides
There may be occasions when you want to print on both sides of a piece of paper. This is very useful for leaflets, newsletters and booklets.

Printing on both sides of paper requires some forethought. You need to plan how you want your document to look when it is printed, because you have to print the odd-numbered pages first and then turn the paper over and print the even-numbered pages.

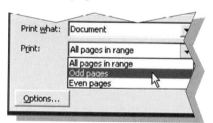

When you have entered all the information into your document, make sure that all the pages are numbered (see pages 44–45). Place the paper in the printer, click on the File menu and select Print. In the bottom left corner of the Print window, select Odd pages from the Print drop-down menu (above). Click on OK to print.

When the pages have printed, turn them over and place them in the printer tray again (see PC Tips, right, for a way of reminding yourself on which side of a sheet of paper your printer prints). Now select

Even pages from the Print drop-down menu in the Print window and click OK. You'll soon have your document printed on both sides of your paper.

● Different weights of paper
Paper comes in many different weights and qualities (the greater the weight and the higher the quality of the paper, the more expensive it is), but most printers can handle a wide range of paper weights.

The weight of paper is measured in grams per square metre, or gsm. Standard printer paper is 80gsm. Paper weight is an important factor when printing at home. Paper that is too thick may jam the printer, so be sure to check your printer manual for the maximum paper weight your printer can handle. Most modern printers can use card, which has a weight of about 200gsm, so you can print greetings, index and business cards.

PC TIPS

Check the print position
Working out which way to put paper or envelopes into a printer can be confusing, particularly if you are working with a strange printer. A simple way of working this out is to mark an 'X'

on one side of the paper and place it in the printer paper feeder with the 'X' facing you. Now type a few words into your word processor and print the page. If the words print on the same side of the paper as the 'X', you now know which way to place the paper when you print your real documents.

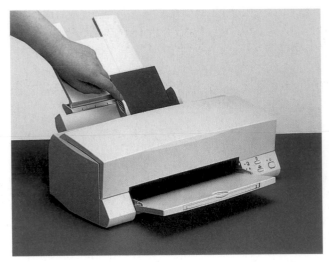

Whatever the size or shape of paper you print on, the only change to make on the printer will be moving the small guides which keep the paper straight as it feeds into the printer.

● Printing on different paper sizes

Most people use standard A4 sheets of paper for their printer, but there are other sizes. Almost all commonly available printers will accept a range of paper sizes from postcards up to A4. If the paper is too small, however, the printer will not be able to feed it through its internal mechanism correctly, so check the printer manual for the minimum paper size usable.

If you are using a colour inkjet printer (see Stage 1, pages 102–103), you can use special paper in a variety of sizes that provides the best quality for printing photographs.

To print on really small paper sizes (the type on which you might print business cards), you will find it easier to use special business card sheets. These comprise a number of cards together on a larger backing sheet that can be fed into a printer.

To print on a different size or shape of paper, you need to change the printing settings. You can do this

while you are using a software program, such as Word. For example, if you want to print a collection of your friends' names and addresses on to separate small index cards, all you have to do is tell Word to expect a different paper size. You do this by clicking on the File menu and selecting the Page Setup option. Choose the Paper tab. In the left of the window, choose from the list of pre-defined paper sizes in the Paper size pull-down menu (below). For other sizes, select the Custom size option and then enter the right measurements in the Width and Height boxes (right, inset)

● Maximum printable area

One important feature in all printers is that you cannot print over the entire sheet of paper. Unprintable

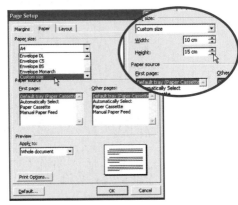

If you are printing on a non-A4 paper size, you should go to the Page Setup window to select the correct size option for your needs.

margins protect the printer from printing on to itself and causing damage to the internal components.

On a laser printer, the margins could be 5mm all the way around the sheet, leaving the printable area within these margins. This margin is set inside your printer and every printer has different margins.

A good way of finding out the maximum printable area of your printer is to ask a program such as Word to tell you. Choose the File menu, then click on Page Setup.

It is possible to achieve superb colour results, even with a glossy finish, using photo-quality inkjet paper.

Click on the Margins tab. In the four margins boxes, type in '0' (zero) as a margin and click on OK. Word will display an error message that warns you that these are not correct margin settings. Click on the Fix button and you will see that Word fills in the minimum margin measurements that can be used with your printer.

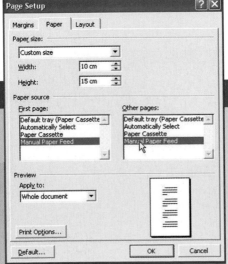

STRAIGHT-THROUGH PAPER PATH

When you print, your printer takes a sheet of paper from the printer tray automatically. On most printers, there is also a manual feed option that lets you feed in sheets of paper, one by one. Why would you use this option?

Laser printers and some inkjet printers feed paper through a complex path of rollers inside the printer. The paper is sent on a twisting and turning route until the

image being printed is formed. Ordinary paper is fine for this, but with envelopes and thicker paper, there's a strong chance that the printer could get jammed.

To avoid this, go to the File menu and select Page Setup, then select the Paper tab. If your printer has a manual feed option, it will include this in the two lists under Paper source, so select them and press the OK button.

Printing an envelope

To give your correspondence a professional-looking appearance, here's how to achieve the perfect end-result.

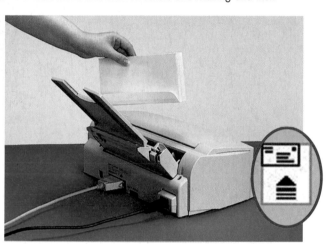

1 As envelopes are generally thicker than normal printing paper, the first point you must address is the risk of the printer jamming. Before you print the envelope, make sure that you adjust the rollers for the thicker paper. This is often achieved simply by using a manually operated lever.

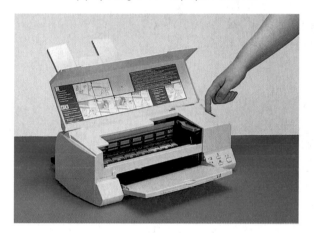

2 Make sure that you place the envelope in the printer the right way up. There may be a sticker or picture on the printer to help you, or you can turn to Word for assistance. Click on the Tools menu and click on Letters and Mailing and then select Envelopes and Labels. In the bottom right of this window there is a picture showing how you should place the envelope in the printer (inset). You might have to remove any paper before you place the envelope on the feeder (refer to your printer manual for advice).

3 The envelopes might be larger or smaller than the paper you were previously using. Either way, you can move one of the guides to accommodate them. Don't make the guides grip the envelopes too tightly, though, or the envelopes won't feed into the printer. With most inkjet printers, the paper or envelopes just rest in the sheet feeder – there is no need to try and make the leading edge of the paper 'engage' in the rollers.

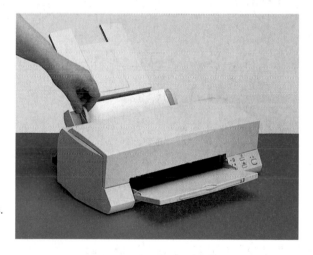

4 Here we can see an envelope coming out of the printer with the address face up. If the address prints on the wrong side of the envelope, you can click on the picture shown on Step 2 (above) and switch between Face up and Face down settings.

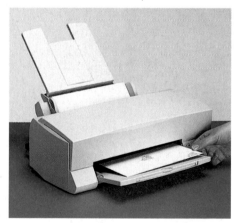

PC TIPS

Window envelopes

If your printer can't handle envelopes or it's too time consuming to change from sheets of paper to envelopes when you want to send a letter, an alternative is to use envelopes with transparent windows. With these you just have to position the recipient's address on the body of the letter so that it shows through the window when the letter is folded and put into the envelope.

5 The envelope is now ready, with the recipient's address clearly displayed and the sender's address in the top left corner. Depending on your printer, you might be able to place a stack of envelopes on the printer's feeder tray or just one, as needed.

Charles MacDonald
55 Southview Drive
Eastcliff-on-Sea
West Sussex
EA9 9YT

Peter Tonkinson
The Sound Studio
Mortimer Road
London
A23 BC45

Controlling inkjet costs

Inkjet printers can produce amazing results – and amazing bills for replacement cartridges! But there are ways of keeping costs down while still getting the most out of your printer.

Inkjet printers are inexpensive to buy, but can be horrendously expensive to run, churning their way through paper and ink at an alarming rate. But there are a number of ways in which you can dramatically cut your printing costs.

First of all, you can cut down on paper costs by using the right paper for the job. The price of paper varies enormously, with the most expensive costing perhaps a hundred times as much as the cheapest. The specially coated paper made by the printer manufacturers, for instance, produces great results but can cost a fortune – typically £10 for 15 sheets, which works out at an amazing 66p per sheet of paper! General inkjet paper costs around a tenth as much. So it makes sense to use the coated paper only when it is absolutely essential for top quality results and to use cheaper paper for all your rough drafts and less important printouts.

● Using copier paper

You can make even greater savings by using general-purpose copier paper, rather than inkjet paper, for drafts. It works perfectly well in most inkjet printers – yet usually costs less than 1p a sheet.

An additional advantage of using copier paper is that you can get it in different colours, or preprinted in a range of varied designs. If you can find the colour or design to suit your taste, this is a much more cost effective option than printing solid colour backgrounds.

● Monitoring ink consumption

You should take the makers' claims about ink consumption with a pinch of salt; the rate at which your printer uses ink depends to a large extent on the kind of pages you print. The makers' figures for ink consumption are often based on just 15 per cent ink coverage per page. If you print lots of pages with solid colour, or full-page photos, you get through ink cartridges much quicker.

One way to cut ink costs is to work out what kind of printing you are doing. Next time you start a new cartridge, make a list with five columns: draft black text, top-quality black text, a little colour, 50 per cent colour and full-page colour. Place a tick in the appropriate column for each page printed. Use a special mark for pages that are reprints with minor changes. You could be reprinting many ink-greedy top quality black text pages if you're only spotting mistakes on the printout. If so, you could print in draft mode first, switching to top quality for the final printout.

There are many ways to cut the cost of inkjet printing so you won't feel constrained about outputting your work.

CHECKPOINT ✔

TOP TIPS TO KEEP YOUR PRINTING COSTS DOWN

☑ Check the document on screen before you print. Use the Print Preview to check for layout errors.

☑ Recycle draft pages. Keep wasted printouts for other drafts, notes or drawing paper.

☑ Keep a record of your total expenditure for your printer.

☑ Use draft mode on your printer. This uses a lot less ink. Save the ink for those important documents.

☑ Shop around for new cartridges. Not only do prices vary from shop to shop, but also you might find a multipack that saves even more.

☑ If you use your printer a lot, consider refilling your cartridges.

Refilling an inkjet cartridge

We show you why you don't necessarily have to buy an expensive new cartridge every time the black or coloured inks run out.

IF YOU USE a lot of ink – two or more cartridges a month – think about using cartridge refill kits. These allow you to replace the ink without throwing the cartridge away.

Printer manufacturers frown on this practice – partly because they make lots of money from the high price of new cartridges. They argue that you might accidentally damage your printer through ink leakage.

However, if you are organized and careful, you can safely refill cartridges several times before replacing them with new ones. Do check that you are not invalidating your printer's

warranty before doing so, however. The refilling process should never be rushed. Take care, because spilt ink can irritate eyes and skin and wreck computer desks and printers. Clear an area where you can work comfortably and have absorbent paper towels ready for any spills. You must refill cartridges as soon as they are empty, or else ink can dry and block the cartridge. Finally, if you are refilling a three-chamber colour cartridge, take extra care to ensure the ink doesn't mix, even in the filler syringe; make sure you wash out the syringe between each colour.

1 Read the maker's instructions carefully and look for any variations specific to your printer. You might have to carefully tape over the holes for the ink cartridge reservoirs with masking tape to stop ink leaking.

2 Turn the cartridge over and, if possible, lever off the first plastic cap with a penknife. If it does not come off easily, locate the ink fillers and bore through the plastic to enlarge them with a small drill or a penknife.

3 Load the syringe with ink and insert the needle halfway into the correct coloured reservoir. You might feel some resistance as many cartridges contain sponge. Then slowly press the syringe plunger to fill the reservoir.

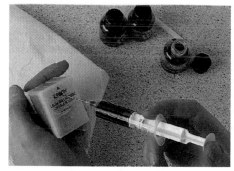

4 Take care not to overfill the reservoir – the maker's instructions should tell you how much to use. Wash out the syringe thoroughly with water between each colour, drawing water in with the plunger and squirting it out into a disposable dish until it runs clear.

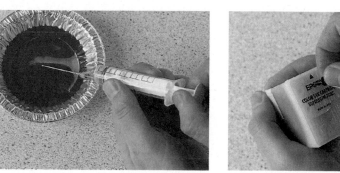

5 When the ink is in the cartridge, seal the reservoirs by inserting the rubber bungs which are supplied with the refill kit into each of the filler holes. Make sure you push these home firmly so that there is no chance of a leak around the sides.

6 Stand the cartridge head down on blotting paper for two minutes to draw out excess ink and equalize cartridge pressure. Check carefully for any leaks. You must never put a leaky cartridge back into your printer. If you can't stop leaks, replace the cartridge.

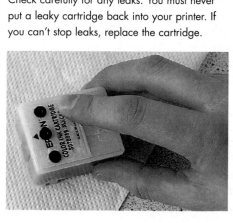

Recordable CDs

The CD has revolutionized both hi-fi and computer markets, offering huge storage capacity at a low price. But now the best thing is that you can write your own CDs!

The Compact Disc is an incredible storage medium. A single CD-ROM can store up to 650MB of data – the equivalent of over 450 floppy disks. To achieve this amazing storage feat, the CD production process stores the 1s and 0s of binary data as tiny pits on the surface of the silver disc inside the CD. When you put the disc into your CD-ROM drive, the sensor in the drive uses laser light to detect the tiny pits and read the information.

However, the name CD-ROM stands for Compact Disc Read Only Memory, which means that the information stored on it cannot be changed: you can read it, but not write to it. Once a pit is pressed into the disc surface during manufacture, it is permanent.

● Ideal CDs

The ideal storage medium is a CD that you can write yourself. This makes backing up important information

With a special CD-R (Recordable CD) drive and disks, massive amounts of computer data can be stored in the form of a code made up of 1s and 0s.

much easier. For example, making a back-up copy of a 6MB picture with floppy disks is very difficult and time-consuming. However, a CD that is also able to record information could store over 100 such pictures before you even had to reach for a second disc.

Recordable CD drives for PCs are available, and they're known as CD-R (CD-Recordable). They comprise two parts: a special CD drive and a CD that can then be read by any CD drive.

There are few restrictions on what can be written to a CD – it could be data, programs, images or even music. The simple rule is that if the information is on your computer's hard disk, then it can be written on a CD-R, without taking up as much physical space as conventional floppies.

CLOSE-UP ON CD DISCS

Look at a CD-ROM disc and a CD-R disc side by side, and you'll spot some immediate differences. The CD-ROM looks silver. One side has a label to indicate what's on the CD. On the flip side, if you look very closely, you should be able to make out the part that contains information (the area closest to the centre should appear slightly darker). Under a microscope, this would look like grooves composed of pits or indentations. The CD-R disc, by contrast, is silver or gold on one side and greeny-blue on the other. The surface of the silver or gold side has a label on which you can write the CD contents. The greeny-blue side shows the recording surface through the clear plastic. Once again, the areas that contain information will appear darker than the other areas. Under a microscope, the surface appears to be flat, but some parts will be shaded by the writing process.

● CD-R drives

Information has to be stored on CD-R discs using a dedicated CD-R drive, as only these have the special lasers that can 'write' to the disc. Normal CD-ROM drives were designed only for reading information, so they lack this writing laser.

The write laser makes changes in a layer of photosensitive dye that the special CD-R discs contain. To write a bit of information, the laser heats up a tiny spot of the dye, which becomes less reflective. If you put the CD-R disc into a normal CD-ROM drive, the bits of information can be read from these spots just as if they were tiny pits in the surface of a normal CD-ROM disc.

● The costs of CD-R

CD-R drives range in price from £70 to £150. Blank CD-R discs cost well under £1 each, and as little as 25p each when bought in packs of 100.

Most CD-R drives include the CD writing software needed to create the CDs. The process in which data is stored on a CD-R disc is very different to that used on a floppy disk. The laser writing process needs a steady stream of data and any interruptions can result in the CD-R disc being rendered unreadable – ruining the disc and requiring you to start the process again. Fortunately, modern CD writing software makes it easy to create your own CDs reliably.

● ReWritable CDs

One of the limitations of CD-R is that it is a strictly 'write once' method. As soon as the write laser has heated a spot on the disc surface, it cannot be changed back to its previous state, so unlike your old hard disk, you cannot simply record over old files.

To tackle this limitation, many CD-R drives also work as CD-RW (or CD ReWritable) drives that allow the user to write and rewrite data to special CD-RW discs. Like the CD-R, these discs have a recording layer that can be altered by a write laser. The difference is that CD-RW discs can go through a special reheating process. This process returns the recording layer to its original state so that it can be written to again.

● The future

The very latest storage medium to use lasers and optical discs is even more impressive. A Digital Versatile Disc (DVD) can store between 4.7 and 17GB (that's 4,700–17,000MB) on a disc the same size as a CD. This is up to 26 times more data than a conventional CD-ROM or CD-R disc.

DVD discs can also store complete movies with better-than-VHS quality and 'surround sound'. You can buy DVD players to connect to your TV, and thousands of movies have been released in DVD format. DVD drives are now fitted as standard on some home PCs. Recordable DVD drives and discs are also emerging – albeit at a hefty price. Conflicting formats for the discs mean that it's too early for most home users to consider but a DVD writer may well be part of your future PC.

Inside a writable CD-R

Layers of a CD-R disc

Label and protective layer – to tell you what's on the CD.
Reflective layer – to reflect the reading laser back.
Writing layer – the layer of photosensitive dye.
Disc substrate – a clear plastic coating to protect the writing layer.

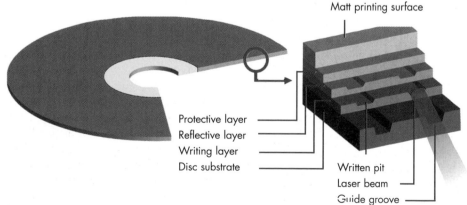

Matt printing surface

Protective layer
Reflective layer
Writing layer
Disc substrate

Written pit
Laser beam
Guide groove

When the CD-R is written

Information is written to a CD-R as a series of 0s and 1s. When a 1 is required, the laser alters the photosensitive dye for that bit of data, creating a darker or less reflective part of the CD-R. When a 0 is required, the laser leaves the dye, and its reflectivity, unaltered.

When the CD-R is read

When the laser moves across part of the CD-R, it reads the less reflective or darker areas as pits or 1s and the reflective, unaltered areas as flats or 0s. In this way, it can read the information that you write to the CD-R as it would any CD.

ADDING A CD-R DRIVE

External CD-R drives are readily available and they normally plug straight into a USB port. They are easy to install, and will come with their own software. Follow the instructions supplied with the device and its software CD to get your computer to recognize the drive.

Next install the software for actually writing your CDs. Again, you will find this easy to follow, and most have a user-friendly interface. If you have any problems, contact the computer store where you bought the writer, and ask for help.

3D graphics cards

If you're a computer games fan, it's worth considering the boost in graphics quality that can be achieved by fitting one of these high-tech add-ons.

The fast graphics chips on 3D graphics cards can draw many millions of shapes each second to create fantastic and sharply detailed moving images.

The quality of graphics in computer games has taken a big leap in the past few years, largely thanks to a new breed of graphics card, often called a 3D accelerator.

These graphics cards have chips dedicated to the task of drawing realistic and absorbing 3D scenes. The main purpose of the 3D accelerator is to calculate and display **polygons**. Since the vast majority of modern PC games take place in 3D polygonal worlds, their graphics get a huge boost from the 3D accelerator.

● The benefits

The improvement is twofold. First, a 3D graphics card increases the polygon power of your PC to such an extent that even a relatively slow computer (such as a 600MHz PC) becomes fast and smooth when running 3D games. Second, it enables the PC to display special effects such as translucent water, lens flare and more detailed textures – all of which add extra realism to the game.

Without a 3D accelerator, a PC's main processor must do much of this complex graphics work itself. With a 3D accelerator, the main processor is free to dedicate itself to tasks such as working out the positions of the players and objects. The result is smooth action in a realistic, absorbing 3D world.

In recent years, 3D graphics cards have become cheaper and more readily available. Many can now be bought for little more than the cost of a couple of games. And if you shop around, you might also find attractive offers, such as a 3D card boxed together with one or more games.

● Games power

This renewed interest in 3D graphics power is largely due to the success of dedicated games consoles, such as the Sony PlayStation 2, Nintendo

---

WHAT IT MEANS

POLYGONS
The 3D world of the modern computer game is made up of many objects created from thousands of much smaller three- or four-sided shapes called polygons. The 3D accelerator card can draw and fill millions of polygons per second – fast enough to create the effect of smooth and realistic animation.

The addition of murky lighting effects and clouds gives action games more atmosphere, and 3D chips can draw such scenes quickly – without burdening the PC's processor.

The 3D graphics chips in Matrox's soon-to-be-released Parhelia remove unwanted jagged edges in a 3D scene but leave the rest of the image sharp and intact.

With Matrox FAA-16x

Without Matrox FAA-16x

Microsoft® Flight Simulator 2002

GameCube and Microsoft X-box. These are able to produce games graphics that are often far superior to those of a standard PC.

The only way for a PC to compete as a games machine is to give it the extra circuitry of a 3D graphics card – similar to the electronics of the consoles – and combine this with the computer's existing processing power.

The reason why a PC needs an add-on to create console-quality graphics is that the PC is, and always has been, a business computer at heart. This means that it's great at calculating tax returns and dealing with thousands of words of text, but has little built-in capacity for displaying moving three-dimensional images.

● **What you get**

The easiest way to get an idea of what 3D cards do is to go to a computer store, play a 3D game and compare its visual effects with and without the enhanced 3D graphics. The pictures of popular games on this page demonstrate how the 3D-enhanced image is much smoother in texture and colouring.

In the two examples of the flying plane above right, notice how the wings of the angled aircraft appear blocky in the standard version (bottom image). In the enhanced version (top image) all the details appear as single, smooth lines. The improvements are even more striking when you actually play a game with

detailed objects and characters, and graphics that move smoothly.

● **Costs**

Graphics chipsets are expensive to develop and manufacture, and the very best gaming performance doesn't come cheap. The Creative 3D Blaster 4 Titanium 4600, with the GeForce4 chipset, costs over £250. Expect the Matrox Parhelia cards to cost even more. If you're on a tighter budget, cards using the GeForce2 chipset are now available for around £70.

Such cards replace your PC's standard graphics card. Installing a 3D accelerator is relatively easy, but as you have to open up your PC to do it, you should get an expert to help you out, or find a dealer who will fit it for you. After the card is fitted, installing the card's software should take only a few minutes.

CARD CHOICE

These days, all 3D cards combine standard 2D functions and 3D acceleration capabilities on one card, so they offer good value to most gamers. The most important factor to look out for is the type of graphics and associated chips – the 'chipset' – the card uses. Manufacturers develop and market new chipsets with increasing frequency, so consider buying the latest and best ones available if and when you decide to go for a 3D card.

One of the latest and fastest such chipsets is the nVIDIA GeForce4, as used in many of today's fastest graphics cards. Such chipsets are aimed not just at providing super-fast gaming, but at enhancing the crucial area of games

graphics known as T&L – transform and lighting – the means by which one scene changes to another and is realistically lit. Other respected chipsets are the Radeon 8500 from ATI and the Parhelia 512 from Matrox. Because of rapid development in the technology, it's well worth quizzing the sales people before you buy a 3D card to ensure that you're not getting one that will quickly be superseded by something better and cheaper. Similarly, bear in mind that games have to be written specifically to take advantage of the improvements in 3D cards, so be sure to ask searching questions about whether a new card actually has many games that show all its features.

The graphics improvement is obvious in Quake II. On a basic PC (above left) the image is jagged and blocky. With a 3D accelerator (above right) it looks smooth.

Alternative input devices

The standard keyboard and mouse are not the only ways of controlling what happens on your screen. If you want to make your computing more fun – or more accurate – try some of the alternatives.

The most powerful and expensive PC components are inside your computer, but they wouldn't be much use to you without the simple and generally cheap components on the outside – the mouse and keyboard. Most people are happy with the mouse and keyboard supplied with their computer at the time of purchase, but you're not stuck with them. If you find the normal keyboard makes typing tedious, or perhaps your young children find it hard to get to grips with the standard mouse, there are alternatives to explore.

Your options include ergonomically shaped keyboards (see Ergonomics, below), a mouse that doesn't need a cable and special pen-based drawing tools.

Even just updating your mouse or keyboard can make work on your computer more efficient and enjoyable.

● Try the alternatives

You might find that the keyboard supplied with your PC becomes uncomfortable with prolonged use. You can easily change it for a better quality one. Some have a specially contoured layout which helps ease fatigue, while others have different key actions. Ask at your local computer shop to see if they'll let you try out the alternatives: you might prefer keyboards with firmer, more positive springing under the keys, while others favour softer keys. You might also like to use an in-built wrist rest.

The Logitech Marble Mouse combines elements from a mouse and a trackball to form a very precise, yet hand-sized, input device.

● Easier mouse-work

The earliest computer users had to make do with only a keyboard for entering information into their computers, which modern PC-users would find unbelievably slow. Since then, the mouse has become an essential PC accessory. A mouse is often the easiest way to access menus, buttons and objects on the screen, but, like the keyboard, some of the

---

ERGONOMICS

The buzzword that has transformed the way you use and interact with a computer is ergonomics. This is the study of the way in which people use machines. It covers everything from the way that you sit at your desk and hold your mouse to the layout of the keyboard and the picture on the monitor. If you get these factors wrong, you'll find a computer is tiring and even painful (headaches, neck-ache or wrist problems are serious concerns for computer users). Ergonomically designed computer accessories are intended to minimize the chances of such problems.

mice supplied with home computers can prove difficult or uncomfortable to use. Don't worry, however, you're not restricted to the standard mouse. As you'll see on this page and the next, there are plenty of alternatives that can make mouse-work easier, more fun and much more accurate to use for drawing and painting programs, such as Microsoft Paint and CorelDRAW.

Trackballs reduce the need for lots of space, cordless mice reduce cable clutter and there are mice specially tailored for young hands. An optical mouse uses a light-sensitive tracking device to plot its position. It is more precise than an ordinary mouse and needs cleaning less often. Artists frustrated by the tricky practice of painting with the mouse can add a special pen and pad to supplement the mouse for more natural artwork.

● The price is right

Many of these alternative accessories are not expensive, so if you're finding your existing components fatiguing, it's worth thinking about changing them. A good-quality keyboard should cost no more than £20, with ergonomically shaped layouts such as Microsoft's Natural Keyboard costing around £35. Keyboards for children start from £15–25.

Surprisingly, a mouse is often more expensive than a keyboard: a high-quality replacement mouse is around £25 and a cordless mouse can cost around £40. For budding designers and artists, a drawing pad and pen starts at £50, and professionals can pay £400 or more for a top-of-the-range pad.

PLUG AND PLAY

Windows XP tries to make it easy for you to install new devices on your computer. When it starts up, Windows looks for new devices that you have added while the PC was switched off. This is called plug and play.

Many keyboards and mice replace existing components without any extra intervention, but you should always check with your computer supplier that any new device you buy is Windows XP and plug-and-play compatible.

Gallery of devices

If you're looking to replace or supplement your keyboard or mouse, here's a round-up of the types of device available. Some are fun, others have more serious uses, but what they all have in common is that they take only around five minutes to add to your computer.

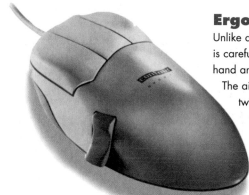

Ergonomic mouse

Unlike an ordinary mouse, the ergonomic version is carefully shaped to fit more precisely into your hand and provide extra comfort and support. The aim is to help mouse users avoid any of the twinges and aches that can afflict people who spend long hours at the computer. The ergonomic mouse is available in different sizes.

Mice with wheels

All but the cheapest and zaniest novelty mice include a central wheel in addition to the left and right mouse buttons. This main purpose of this wheel is to make it easy to scroll through documents and Web pages. Instead of having to move the mouse to a program's scroll bars, you simply roll the wheel back and forwards to move the page.

Art pad and pen

If you've been following the Paint and CorelDRAW exercises in *PCs made easy* you might have found that painting with the mouse can be tricky. The best option to improve your artwork is a drawing pad that works with a special pen. As you move the pen over the pad, its position is detected by sensors in the pad and translated into signals that control the pointer on the screen.

The great benefit of a drawing pad is that it feels and works just like a pen and paper. Some pads even detect pressure for special effects, such as controlling the amount of paint put down on the picture.

USB mouse

Traditionally, a mouse was connected to your PC's serial port or PS/2 socket, but the widespread adoption of the USB (Universal Serial Bus) interface gives you an additional and welcome connection option if your PC has USB sockets. The USB standard supports 'hot plugging', meaning that you do not have to turn the computer on or off if you swap the device, as it is immediately recognized and ready for work. Using a USB mouse also means that you do not run the risk of tying up your only serial port, which might be more usefully employed for a modem or other device.

HANDWRITING RECOGNITION

Understandably, many new computer users would rather use handwriting to put words into a computer than learn to type. Despite this demand, however, handwriting recognition has failed to make its mark in mainstream desktop computing.

While handwriting recognition sounds useful, most of the handwriting recognition software requires you to learn a slightly newer way of writing words. It's also not 100 per cent accurate – which rather works against the benefits of handwriting recognition.

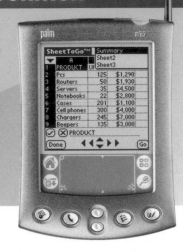

Gyroscopic mouse

This kind of mouse doesn't even have to be used on a flat surface. The gyroscopic mouse works by sending a radio signal to a base unit that can measure the distance of the mouse away from the computer – even when it's in the air and not on a desk. The gyroscopic mouse can also be used in a more conventional way by rolling it on the desk, or using a built-in trackball.

Marble Mouse

This looks like a mouse with a big ball in it. Rotate the ball with your index finger to move the cursor on screen. It saves space and is more precise than an ordinary mouse.

Cordless mouse

One of the problems with a standard mouse is that its cord keeps getting tangled up. One solution is to use a cordless mouse, which has a small base unit that plugs into your computer. As you move the mouse, it sends a signal to the base station to move the pointer. Some cordless mice use an infra-red light beam (like a TV remote control); these require a clear, unobstructed path to the base unit. Mice that use radio signals are not so fussy and can work on a cluttered table.

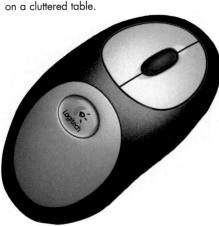

Novelty mice

Some mice are simple redesigns of standard mice, with bright colours and bigger buttons. If you are ever stuck for a present, this type of mouse certainly makes a great novelty gift.

SPEECH RECOGNITION

It may sound like science fiction, but you can also control your computer by talking to it. A modern home PC is capable of listening to your voice (picked up by the microphone) and converting your words into commands. Speech recognition is only held back by the processing speed of the computer, but any PC able to run Windows XP has enough power to produce impressive results. Already, voice-recognition programs let you choose menu commands and dictate text into word processors and other documents.

As this technology progresses, the potential for physically impaired computer users will also develop.

Upgrading to a cordless mouse

It's easy to add a new input device to your computer. Here's your step-by-step guide to installing one of these devices – a tangle-free cordless mouse.

1 If the input device you are adding uses anything other than a USB socket (see Sockets, below), you must first switch your PC off to perform the upgrade. If you are upgrading to a USB-style input device – such as the Logitech cordless mouse used here – you can leave the PC switched on and go directly to Step 2.

2 Insert the plug for the new device into the appropriate socket on the back of the PC. USB plugs can go into any unused USB socket, but PS/2 plugs must be fitted into their own colour-coded socket: green for the mouse and blue for the keyboard.

3 With USB devices, Windows detects your new hardware and sets it up automatically. For non-USB devices, switch the PC on and Windows will detect it when it starts up. If the device included a software CD-ROM, install the software now. Then just set up the new input device on your desktop. For this cordless mouse, the receiver is placed at the back of the desk and the mouse is free to roam anywhere in front of the receiver.

MULTIPLE INPUT DEVICES

Windows can handle several input devices at the same time. Of course, only one mouse pointer appears on the screen, but you can choose which device to use to control it. For example, you can use trackball alongside a conventional mouse, using whichever one best suits the task in hand.

Many graphics artists use a tablet and pen together with a mouse to get the best of both worlds.

SOCKETS

Whatever type of input device you decide on, you must check the sockets available on your PC. Mice usually have a PS/2 or a USB plug, and most keyboards use a PS/2 or a USB plug. PC design is gradually changing over from PS/2 plugs and sockets to USB plugs and sockets. For this reason, it makes most sense to buy USB-equipped input devices wherever possible. Just make sure that your PC has a spare USB socket. A few input devices come with simple PS/2 to USB adapters so that you can use them with either type of socket.

A few devices, such as low-cost art pads, work alongside your mouse and keyboard. If you are not replacing an existing device, look to see if there is a spare socket for it on your PC's back panel.

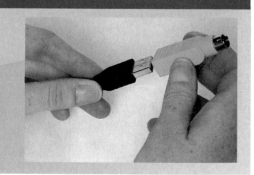

Taking control of your games

If you want to play games to win, you need the right control tool for the job. Add a joystick or steering wheel to your PC for fine control over flying and racing games.

The sheer versatility of your PC's keyboard and mouse makes them perfect for some games, especially those that are strategy based. But, for hands-on games, joysticks, steering wheels and gamepads give you greater control and greater involvement too.

● Keyboard and mouse

The keyboard has over 100 keys, which is good for complex games. It is a digital device, which means that the switches are either on or off. This works well if you just want to fire a missile, but not when you need finer control over some aspect of your game – when you're playing a flight simulator and you want to angle the plane slightly left, for example. Keyboards often work best with simpler strategy games.

● Joystick

There are two types of gaming joysticks: digital and analog. Digital joysticks move in one of eight directions like the eight main points on a compass. This kind of joystick is rare with PCs and is generally used only on arcade machines. With PCs, the norm is analog joysticks, shaped like those used to control real fighter aircraft. Not surprisingly, they are mostly used for flight simulators, but can also

Joysticks like Microsoft's SideWinder Force Feedback2 are the last word in game control, giving realistic 'feel' with force feedback.

work with racing or 3D adventure games. With analog control, the movements on the screen more accurately mirror the movements you put into the joystick. For example, moving the joystick a little way gives a correspondingly small movement on screen; moving it a long way gives a large movement on screen.

● Types and prices

Joystick prices vary considerably. A simple two-button model can cost up to £20, but a state-of-the-art, multi-buttoned Force Feedback joystick can cost up to £60.

Less common are the throttle sticks used as add-ons by some flight simulator fans to help accentuate the feeling of flying. They look like aeroplane throttles studded with buttons, but they are expensive at around £50 or so. Serious gamers can opt for two-handed flight sticks, known as yokes. These work in the same way as joysticks, but they are expensive (at around £80), due to their more complex construction. They are more true-to-life for non-combat flight simulators, however, and provide a realistic steering wheel. Gamepads do the same job for PCs as those that are used on television

game consoles, from Nintendo to Sony. They are ideal for simple action games, such as beat-'em-up games. Some people don't like the feel of the directional pad, so with most you can fix a small joystick instead. These are inexpensive devices, and you can usually buy one for £10–20.

● Steering wheel

Just as there are joysticks for flight simulators, so there are steering wheels to heighten the realism of motor-racing games.

For the ultimate in racing game control, you can also get a steering wheel with an additional brake and accelerator pedal to go on the floor under your desk. Simple steering wheels are available for around £40 – but you should expect to pay a much higher price for the more sophisticated versions.

WHAT IT MEANS

FORCE FEEDBACK

A new technology for many types of joystick is called force feedback. This is an attempt to bring the realism of the bigger 'sit down' arcade machines to the home computer user. For example, in a flight simulator, the joystick could actually push back to represent the physical stresses a pilot feels. It might be more difficult to turn in a tight corner, or become almost uncontrollable during a crash. CH Products and Microsoft make joysticks using this technology, and steering wheels are also available.

Setting up a joystick in Windows

Even with a basic joystick, action-packed games can be easier to play and more fun. Once you've plugged in a new joystick you have to set it up to work properly by running a simple calibration process.

ADDING A NEW joystick or steering wheel is easy. If your joystick has a USB plug, you simply plug it into an unused USB port on your PC and follow the on-screen instructions when Windows automatically detects the device. This makes it appear in the Game Controllers panel

(see Step 5, below). Many low-cost joysticks have a 15-pin plug that fits into the joystick/MIDI socket that's on the back of almost all PCs. To fit this type of joystick, switch off your PC and then plug the joystick in. Switch back on and then follow the full setup procedure shown below.

1 Select Control Panel from the Start menu. The Control Panel window appears.

2 Double-click the icon labelled Game Controllers and the special Game Controllers dialog box will appear.

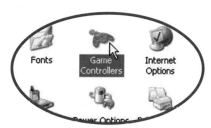

3 Unless you already have a joystick installed, the main panel of the dialog box will be blank. Click the Add button to begin setting up your joystick.

4 A new dialog box will appear with a long list of joysticks (and other types of game controllers) on it. If the name of your joystick appears on this list, select it and click the OK button. If your joystick does not appear in the list, look through the leaflet that came with your joystick for a description of its type; this is usually given as the number of axes and buttons. Select the appropriate description and click the OK button.

5 The name of your joystick (or its type) appears in the central panel of the Game Controllers dialog box. At this point, Windows will recognize that your joystick is installed, but in order to make the most of it, you will have to **calibrate** it. Click the Properties button to begin this process.

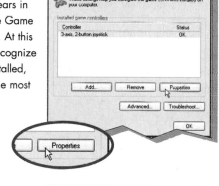

6 The Test tab of the next dialog box shows the joystick's functions (this varies from model to model). Try each control and button in turn and make sure that you see the indicators on the screen respond.

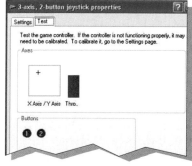

7 It's likely that even when everything works fine, your joystick isn't centred perfectly in the X Axis/Y Axis box. Release the joystick – if the crosshairs don't return to the centre of this box, click on the Settings tab and then click the Calibrate button.

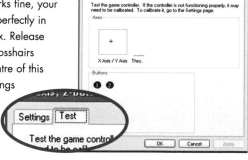

8 A Device Calibration Wizard leads you through the rest of the process. It asks you to try the full range of movement and then adjusts the way Windows interprets the joystick data to correct the minor misalignment. When the Wizard is done, click the OK button. Your joystick is now ready to use.

WHAT IT MEANS

CALIBRATE
When you calibrate your joystick, Windows is measuring its capabilities. The signal emitted by joysticks varies between models so measuring ensures that the programs on your PC can use the full range of movement of the stick.

Upgrading your PC

Your PC is built from components that you can replace to make it go faster. Often, upgrading doesn't even require you to open up the PC.

Is your software running slowly? Is your hard disk groaning under the weight of your files or do you long for a bigger and better monitor so you can see more of the image shown on screen? If so, you should upgrade your PC to take advantage of the latest developments in hardware technology.

This is especially important as your PC gets older: if you want to use the latest software, you might find that it runs slowly on a two-year-old computer, for example. Upgrading for extra performance is one of the most common reasons to spend more on your computer.

● Extra capabilities
Upgrading to add new capabilities to your PC is also important. Have you ever made a back-up copy of your documents? If not – perhaps it's because you just can't squeeze copies of your documents on to a floppy disk – think what might happen if your PC went wrong and you lost all your files.

When you need to keep back-up copies of larger files, such as photographs and sound files, you should consider getting a more capable back-up device, such as a tape drive or a Zip drive (see opposite). These devices plug into the back of your PC and let you copy huge amounts of information for safe-keeping.

If you have been using your PC for graphics, then you are likely to have found that working within the confines of a standard 15- or 17-inch monitor

is awkward. This size of display might be fine for word processing, but with many other types of program, you'll find it easier to work with a bigger monitor. If you opt for a bigger monitor, you'll find it just plugs into the same socket as the old one, so it's easy to add.

● Built for change
One of the best features of your computer is that it is designed for a life of upgrades. Just about every component can be upgraded to keep up with new technology. You can raise the capacity of your hard disk, improve sound quality with a new

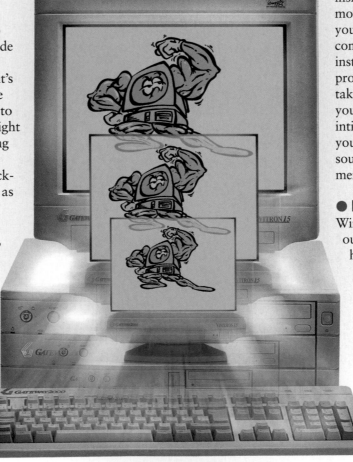

sound card, increase the main memory, plug in new speakers, a bigger monitor or a back-up drive. And because the PC uses standard connections, most upgrade accessories use the same type of cable, making them easier to install.

There are two types of upgrade you can carry out on your PC. The first is to add a new accessory that simply plugs into the back of your computer and covers upgrades such as, for example, a new mouse, modem or speakers. You don't need to be a technical wizard to install this type of upgrade and, fortunately, you don't even have to open up your computer!

The second type of upgrade fits inside your computer and needs more work and time to install; you will need to open up your computer and follow the installation instructions and procedures carefully. When you take the case off and look inside your computer, it might look intimidating, but if you're careful you can quite easily install a new sound card or some extra memory, for example.

● Help at hand
Windows XP is designed to look out for new and upgraded hardware. When you have fitted a new upgraded component, Windows will automatically try to detect it and attempt to set it up for you, making it much easier to get the new upgrade working. Some upgrade components need special software – called driver or controller software – to allow them to function properly, but this will be supplied in the box on either a

floppy disk or CD-ROM. To minimize the chance of finding that a new piece of hardware doesn't work with your computer, look for an upgrade that is clearly labelled as compatible with Windows XP.

Some hardware lacks the drivers needed for Windows XP, and therefore will only work with earlier versions of Windows. If in doubt ask the computer shop for advice before buying. Several years ago, upgrading was a minefield, but now PC manufacturers make it as easy as possible to fit, install and set up your new upgrade.

One of the best developments is a feature called plug and play (see page 105). If your PC has this (and all new PCs do), then you will find upgrading a breeze. Simply plug in the new adapter card, modem or back-up drive and Windows will do the rest for you.

Popular upgrades for your computer

Here's a brief introduction to the main types of upgrade you can add to your home computer. Later in the course, we'll show you how to carry out these upgrades with simple step-by-step instructions.

Memory

One of the best ways to improve the performance of your computer is to fit more main memory (normally called RAM). If your PC has the bare minimum of 64MB of RAM needed for Window XP, you will find a dramatic improvement in speed if you upgrade to 128MB. If you can afford to upgrade to 256MB, you'll get even more speed – especially for graphics programs. You might need some help in choosing the right memory chip (ask the original supplier of your PC for help), but fitting it is straightforward, even though it requires you to open your computer.

Sound card and speakers

To play sound, your PC needs to have a sound card fitted and loudspeakers plugged into the sound card. If you already have a sound card, you can easily upgrade the loudspeakers that plug into a socket on the back of your PC. Upgrading to speakers that include a sub-woofer will improve the quality of the sound your computer pumps out –

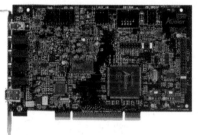

especially for games and music. If you're serious about making music, upgrading to a sound card with better sound quality is worthwhile, although it does require you to open up the PC.

Zip drive

One of the most boring computing jobs is making back-up copies of your files. It's so boring that many home computer users don't bother. However, if you don't make regular back-ups, you might lose all your files if your PC develops a fault. The Iomega Zip drive stores over 250MB of data. That's as much as 170 ordinary floppy disks. A Zip drive simply plugs into the back of your PC. You need only install the driver software.

Bigger monitor

Many home PCs are supplied with a 15- or 17-inch monitor. If you want to use desktop publishing or graphics software, a bigger monitor is better, as you're able to see more of the image. The monitor plugs into the socket at the back of the PC. Once fitted, a simple adjustment to the display settings will make the most of it.

HOW DIFFICULT IS UPGRADING?

Upgrading your computer can be easy, but for some upgrades it is more complex and you'll need to follow any supplied instructions carefully. As a general rule of thumb, if you do not need to open your computer to fit the upgrade, it should be easy to add.

If you do need to open the PC case, then it is likely to be trickier. If you're at all worried about performing the upgrade yourself, consider getting a local computer shop to do it for you. It will cost more, but the peace of mind is well worth it.

CD writer

Adding a CD-R drive (sometimes called CD writer or CD burner) to your PC is a great upgrade. In addition to being able to create your own music CDs – perhaps creating a compilation CD of your all-time favourites – it also helps when you want to back up your documents. It can store 650MB – equivalent to over 450 floppy disks. While there are external CD-R drives, they're less common and usually more expensive; most fit internally.

Home Learning & Leisure

Super science

An understanding of science is a key part of everybody's education, but many people find the whole subject uninspiring and difficult. However, with the help of your computer, learning about science has never been so much fun – and such little hard work.

For many people the very word 'science' conjures up images of dull chemistry lessons and impenetrable physics equations. But science is a vast subject covering many areas of study and so most people should find a topic to interest them, provided it is presented in an inspiring and entertaining way.

This is where that wonder of modern science – your computer – comes in! It can take advantage of the most basic of scientific principles – light and sound – to turn your home into a science wonderland.

There is a great selection of science CD-ROMs available, all of which aim to explore the subject in a new and exciting way. These cover almost every aspect of science and cater for all age groups and abilities, from the absolute beginner to the dedicated professional.

Children in particular will benefit from science-based CD-ROMs. There are programs available to teach young children about the world around them; programs to teach older children the basics of science;

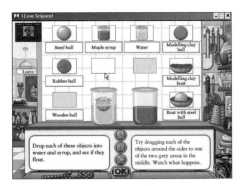

With a lively combination of cleverly presented reference material, interactive experiments, quizzes and other activities, I Love Science! will grip young scientific minds.

and programs to encourage both children and adults to explore the applications of scientific knowledge.

● Junior scientists

Surf into Science 1 is aimed at children as young as four years of age. With the help of Little Blue the whale and his friends, it teaches them some of the basic scientific

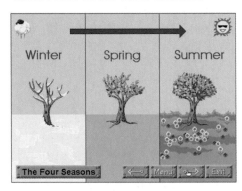

Young children will find basic scientific concepts easy to grasp with the help of the clear graphics, voice-overs and fun visual quizzes in Surf into Science 1.

principles of the world around them. Motion, forces, living and non-living things, growth and seasons are all presented in a simple, accessible way, with clear, colourful images, careful narration and fun, interactive quizzes and games. A second CD-ROM, *Surf into Science 2*, aimed at children aged 7–9, follows a similar format and covers ecology, rocks and fossils, light and sound, colours and propulsion.

● Science and games

The Dorling Kindersley *I Love Science!* CD-ROM is aimed at the 7–11 age group. This lively program has colourful, cartoon-style graphics which encourage children to discover

scientific principles for themselves through experiments and activities. These are performed in three interactive science labs – Rosie's Treehouse, Mo's Workshop and Al's Kitchen – each fronted by a friendly animated character who guides the children through the available options with a seemingly never-ending supply of jaunty banter.

Each lab covers different topics, from energy and forces to materials, the human body, plants, animals and

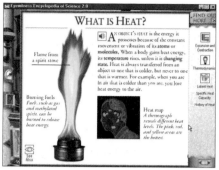

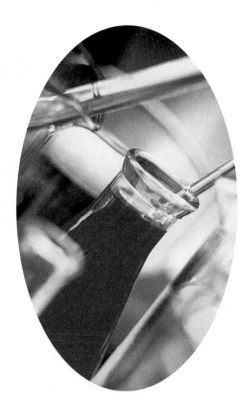

The Dorling Kindersley Eyewitness Encyclopedia of Science 2.0 is dedicated to bringing science to life using sound, video, animation and powerful cross-referencing facilities. It also imparts knowledge using combinations of text, sound and video. Hot links and a Find Out More panel make finding answers easy.

the environment. There are over 100 activities to choose from, with background information, quizzes that check comprehension and interesting 'Did You Know?' facts relating to each one. There is a lot of information on this CD–ROM and children do need to be able readers to get the best from it, but once they start the activities, they'll be hooked.

● Eyewitness science

For older children there is the Dorling Kindersley *Eyewitness Encyclopedia of Science 2.0*, a full Multimedia program combining video with pictures, animation and sound. The information on this disc is grouped under four main subjects: mathematics, physics, chemistry and life sciences. Each of the four

subjects divides into a number of topics. Physics, for example, breaks down into time, atoms, matter, sound, magnetism, force and motion, light, electricity, machines, energy and heat. Each of these, in turn, contains a wide variety of informative articles.

In addition to the broad topic areas, there are four other sections: Earth and the universe, the periodic table, a who's who and a quiz. The who's who offers short biographies of famous scientists from all periods of history. There are explanations of scientific terms and links to additional related material. The biography of Darwin, for example, has a link to his round-the-world voyage aboard *HMS Beagle*, which inspired him to write *The Origin of Species*. If you have an Internet connection, you can also visit the encyclopedia's online science site.

● Origins of the universe

Other science titles explore the work of individual scientists. There is, for example, a Multimedia version of Stephen Hawking's best-selling book *A Brief History of Time*. In this book, Hawking explores some of the most difficult areas of modern physics, suggesting answers to some of the most often asked questions about the universe: where did it come from and where is it going? Did the universe have a beginning and, if so,

Did the universe begin with a 'Big Bang' and will it end in a 'Big Crunch'? These are only two of the fundamental questions that Professor Stephen Hawking seeks to answer in his A Brief History of Time, which also includes an appreciation of the work of past astronomers, such as Ptolemy and Edwin Hubble.

what happened before then? What is the nature of time? Will it ever come to an end? His book isn't the easiest of reading and some of Hawking's 'simplified' explanations are far from simple, but the subject is fascinating and this CD-ROM uses diagrams and illustrations to expand on the text of the book and clarify his theories.

Science on your computer

Physics and chemistry can be tricky subjects, and when exams start to loom, they often seem positively daunting. It's at times like these that science CD-ROMs can help students of all ages.

In GCSE Physics from Europress, there are even mini-assignments to complete after-hours, such as trying to spot the Titan moon with binoculars.

Back in Stage 1 we saw how maths exams can be conquered with the help of your PC (see Stage 1, pages 116–119). In just the same way, unravelling the mysteries of science can be made easier with the advantages of computer-based study.

The way that Multimedia can be used to enhance a previously dull subject is just one of the many reasons why the computer can be an inspiring learning tool – even for the most reluctant student.

● Time for science
Ideally, an educational CD-ROM should be structured around the modern GCSE curriculum, so that it

follows the same modular structure taught in schools. In this way, while students can use a CD-ROM in parallel with their lessons – which can be a refreshingly different style of

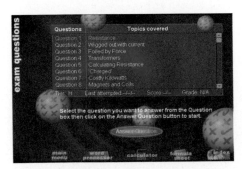

Even though Multimedia educational CD-ROMs have lots of special effects to draw upon, their main aim is to make those real-life exam questions less daunting.

learning – they can also easily concentrate on any areas where they might be having difficulty when they are revising for exams.

● Studying for physics GCSE
GCSE Physics from Europress covers the complete syllabus. Physics is a subject that can be, potentially, very dry, so the publishers have tried to make the contents of the CD-ROM as lively and interactive as possible.

The major subject categories are broken down into easily accessible sub-groups and then broken down further again. With a total of more than 150 topics, the confused student is able to get right to the heart of any problem area.

● Taught by history
Each of the distinct topics in this guide is taught by a famous historical scientific figure: for example, electricity and magnetism is taught by Benjamin Franklin; energy by James

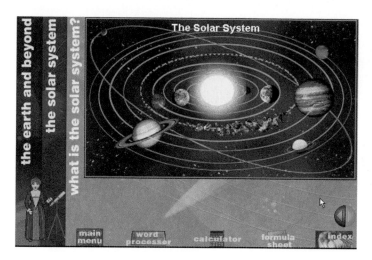

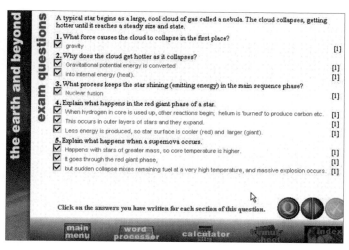

The astronomer Caroline Herschel worked with her famous brother, Sir William Herschel, and, on her own, detected eight comets in the years 1786 to 1797. Now, she will guide you round the universe in the Earth and Beyond section of the GCSE Physics CD-ROM.

When the student has had fun and studied with the historical figure in each section, it's time to find out how much has been remembered. The results of each test can be stored and the student's progress monitored.

Prescott Joule; the Earth and beyond by Caroline Herschel; seismic waves by Zhang Heng; and radioactivity by Sir Ernest Rutherford. Each has his or her own mini-biography – in case you need to be reminded who they are! As you work through a particular module, interactive diagrams pop up to explain things, such as how an electric motor works, for example.

A menu at the bottom of the screen offers convenient functions as you study: an impressive scientific calculator; a word processor that links to Windows WordPad; and a formula sheet with a categorized summary of every formula you could possibly need, from electric currents to thermal energy transfer. There's also an on-screen crib-sheet, which makes an excellent revision resource.

Finally, there are the exams. Each section has a selection of questions that you can look at on-screen. You can complete them as many times as

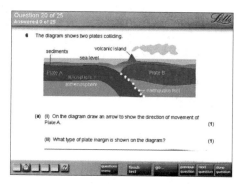

An important feature offered by most tutorial CD-ROMs is the ability to see how you are doing and collate your results over a period of time to track your progress.

you wish and the software remembers your score, grading you accordingly.

● **Serious chemistry**
Moving on to chemistry, *Letts Revise for GCSE Chemistry*, from GSP, contrasts with Europress' friendly guide by focusing directly on the knowledge needed to pass the GCSE exam. Covering the real nitty-gritty of the chemistry syllabus, there are few effects to distract students from the topics. Written by GCSE examiners, it's a text-packed revision aid with basic illustrations and a few animations to illustrate the key points.

When starting the program for the first time, the student must set up a revision plan, based on the start date, the date of the exam, the number of subjects being taken and the number of hours of revision planned in each week. The program uses these figures to suggest dates for progress reviews and practice exam papers. Should students slip up in the test, the program gives a list of topics that need to be brushed up on.

The emphasis is clearly on helping motivated students to pass the exam, rather than presenting chemistry in a fun way. Reinforcing the results-oriented nature of the CD-ROM, GSP offers an A*ABC Guarantee

Letts Revise for GCSE Chemistry is a results-driven and text-heavy approach to exam revision for motivated students, with few Multimedia thrills.

with the software. If your child doesn't get a C or higher GCSE grade at the exam, GSP gives you a £50 voucher to exchange against other GSP titles. The CD-ROM also includes mock examination papers to print out for more realistic exam practice.

CONTACT POINTS

GCSE Physics
Price: £14.99*
Europress
Tel: 01625 855 000
www.europress.co.uk

Letts Revise for GCSE Chemistry
Price: £19.99*
GSP
Tel: 01480 496 666
www.gsp.cc   *UK prices

Amazing space

Astronomy is a subject that has fascinated people for thousands of years. Although anyone with a pair of binoculars can enjoy the wonders of the night skies, if you use your computer, you can see even further into the mysteries of space.

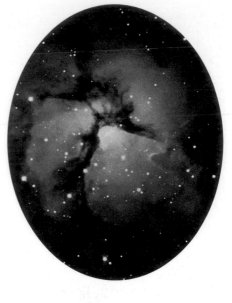

With the help of your PC, the universe is within your grasp. You can simulate the night sky as it is now and discover what those tiny pinheads of light are called and how far away they are. You can travel into the past or the future to view the sky as a Roman legionary did or as it will be seen by your great grandchildren.

You can journey across the surface of Mars or travel to the furthest reaches of the universe. You can learn about gravity and black holes or explore some of the most fascinating questions ever asked, such as what is at the end of the universe and can time flow backwards? Multimedia lets you do all this in ways impossible in a book or on television or video.

● Be an eyewitness
Astronomy software titles range from those designed for enquiring young minds to near-professional standard astronomers. For example, the Dorling Kindersley *Eyewitness Encyclopedia of Space and the*

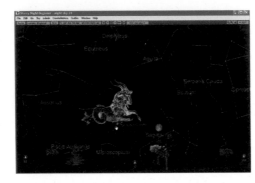

Universe is designed for children aged 10 and up. It provides a good knowledge base of the history of astronomy, space itself and the story of humankind's battle to conquer it.

● A star is born
The *Eyewitness Encyclopedia* is packed with information about astronomers and astronauts, stars and planets, meteors and asteroids, and all the other remarkable phenomena in the universe. You can watch animations of a star being born and the formation of a black hole. You can even find out what it's like to live on a space station.

No matter where you live, you can find out when and where to look for the planets and stars with the help of the Starry Night Beginner CD-ROM (left).

There is a virtual observatory where you can view the night sky from anywhere on Earth and see how the sky changes as you move location. You can even travel through time to see how the sky would have looked 5,000 years ago, or how it will appear to observers 5,000 years in the future.

The wonderful thing about astronomy CD-ROMs is that

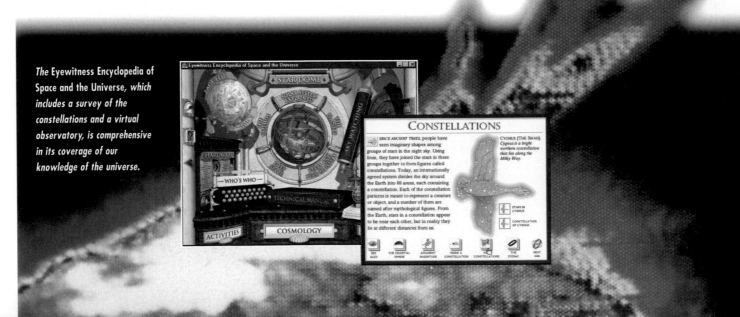

The Eyewitness Encyclopedia of Space and the Universe, which includes a survey of the constellations and a virtual observatory, is comprehensive in its coverage of our knowledge of the universe.

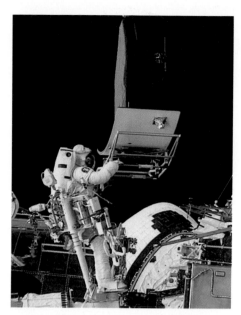

Freed of the optical interference of the Earth's atmosphere, the Hubble space telescope has given astronomers their clearest views yet of the universe. Here, an astronaut carries out repairs on the telescope.

they are available for different age groups, yet they can be enjoyed by all the family. This is most true when looking at general astronomy guides and at CD-ROMs that seek to explain the mysteries of the universe.

● **The night sky**
An excellent beginner's guide to astronomy is *Starry Night Beginner* by Guildsoft Limited, a desktop planetarium designed for all the family. This CD-ROM allows you to view the sky at any time of day or night, anywhere in the world, from 200BC to AD3000, and by setting up your home location when the program first opens you'll see the sky as you do from your own home. Using a simple 'point-and-click' methods, you can identify 100,000

Pilot your own starship to the outer reaches of the universe in **Deep Space Explorer.**

stars, planets and constellations and bring up breathtaking full-screen images of deep-sky galaxies and nebulae. You can also print out customized star charts to help you with your outdoor observations of the real night sky.

● **The solar system and beyond**
Deep Space Explorer, from the same publisher, is far more ambitious in its scope, allowing you to travel anywhere within 700 million light years of Earth – either as an observer or as the pilot of your own intergalactic starship, complete with controls and simulated motion.

This truly impressive program has a database of 28,000 galaxies at its core, all accurately sized and positioned to give an amazing 3D model of the universe. When you start up *Deep Space Explorer* you'll find yourself just beyond the Milky Way, 700,000 light years from home. You can choose to explore or find a specific object in space, using the Heads-up Display to identify any objects as you pass them.

All this is complemented by over an hour of video clips and narration on topics as diverse as satellites and black holes, to help you learn about the universe.

● **Advanced astronomy**
An equally sophisticated virtual observatory with a slightly more academic interface comes in the form of *RedShift*. There are two versions available: *RedShift 3* and the enhanced *RedShift 4*.

Like the *Eyewitness Encyclopedia* and *Starry Night Beginner,* both versions allow you to view the night sky from anywhere on Earth and at any time, from way back in the past to far ahead in the future. Both give access to up-to-the-minute information on what to look for in the real night sky and allow you to penetrate millions of light years into space to experience the wonders of the cosmos at close quarters. There's also a series of Multimedia tutorials on a range of astronomical topics – from the history of the solar system to the theory of the Big Bang and the search for extraterrestrial life.

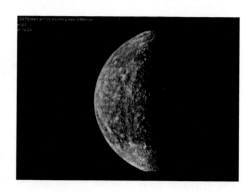

Travel through space with RedShift 4 and see spectacular images of the planets, such as this view of Mercury.

There are detailed, annotated surface maps of Mars, Venus and the Moon, and surface maps for other moons and planets, together with a gallery of spectacular astro-photographs. Both versions also include the comprehensive *Penguin Dictionary of Astronomy.*

The updated *RedShift 4* shares many of the features of *RedShift 3,* but has a superior database, combining the very latest orbital theories with extended star and galaxy catalogues to deliver a highly accurate presentation of the universe. A new interface gives greater control over how you view the universe, and a multiple window facility means you can analyse cosmic events from several different locations at once.

CONTACT POINTS

DK Eyewitness Encyclopedia of Space and the Universe
Price: £19.99*
GSP
Tel: 01480 496 666
www.gsp.cc

Starry Night Beginner
Price: £19.99*
Deep Space Explorer
Price: £39.95*
Guildsoft Limited
Tel: 01752 895 100
www.guildsoft.co.uk

RedShift 3
Price: £9.99*
RedShift 4
Price £19.99*
Focus Multimedia
Tel: 01889 570 156
www.focusmm.co.uk   *UK prices

Learn French the Multimedia way

French is a language that many of us study but few of us master. However, the range of helpful CDs available makes learning effective and fun.

Nearly all of us spend some years at school learning French, and the majority of us forget almost all of it once we have left. Trying to recover what you once learnt by using a book is hard work. The addition of cassettes so that you can listen to dialogues and copy pronunciation is a step forward, but is still not ideal. The Multimedia CD-ROM, however, seems to provide the perfect medium for language-learning on your own; it can store huge amounts of data in the form of text, still or animated images and, crucially, sound.

Multimedia CD-ROMs can offer interactive practice sessions, with hints, tips and exercises to measure your progress. The CDs available for learning French show that software designers are well aware of the possibilities and are exploiting them with a high degree of success.

● French for everyone

If your French is very rusty or you've never attempted to learn the language

At the heart of Mindscape's French for Everyone is the Language Studio, where you can choose from a series of themed lessons. Each lesson is led by your virtual teacher, who also monitors your progress.

Short video clips showing people conversing in real-life situations form the core of the lessons in French for Everyone. The emphasis is on teaching language that you'll find useful as a visitor.

before, it's worth considering *French for Everyone*, one of the most ambitious Multimedia courses available. Aimed at anyone planning to travel to France on holiday or business, the program consists of three CD-ROMs and an accompanying themed phrase book which can be used as a prompt in the interactive conversations you'll take part in.

A Multimedia version of the traditional language course, the emphasis is on understanding and speaking, and you'll need to have a microphone enabled to participate in the exercises.

The program is built around eight core lessons, which take place in the Language Studio. These are presented by your virtual teacher and range from arrival, getting around, meeting people, eating out and shopping, to unexpected events.

Each lesson follows the same pattern: first you'll be introduced to key words and phrases, which you can record and play back; then you'll see a short video of a conversation, which you can view with or without a written translation; and finally there are quizzes that test your comprehension. The program incorporates a sophisticated speech recognition engine which tells you how good your pronunciation is and assesses whether your spoken answers are correct.

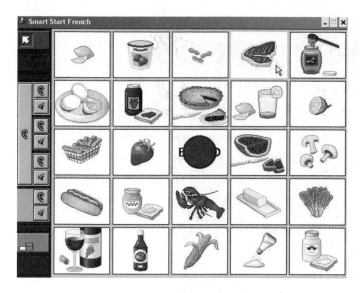

Teaching-you French includes some fast-moving quizzes and games to improve comprehension. Typically, a series of clues is given to help you to identify an object.

The comic-strip conversation in the advanced level of Teaching-you French allows you to listen, take the part of one of the characters and learn French grammar.

Once you have worked through a lesson, you can put your knowledge to the test in the Travel Lab, where you'll interact face-to-face with French speakers in simulated situations that mirror the lessons. Vocabulary and dialogue can be reinforced by playing on the games machines in the Games Room and an English-French/French-English dictionary is always on hand, wherever you are in the program, along with a grammar book to help with any queries.

● Learning by immersion

Another program that gives you plenty of opportunity to practise spoken French is *Teaching-you French* from Focus Multimedia. Focusing on a combination of listening, reading and speaking skills, it completely immerses you in the

Ecoutez! relies on a series of simple point-and-click word games to develop vocabulary and understanding. The language is fairly advanced.

language – there are no English translations along the way!

Again, you'll need a microphone to participate in the spoken exercises, and the program's speech recognition technology evaluates your pronunciation and enables you to record and play back your speech to compare yourself with the voice of the native speaker.

● Fun and games

This is a fun approach to learning, with games and activities graded in three levels of increasing competence: vocabulary, phrases and finally conversations. You choose a subject (food, numbers, people, activities and so on) and a mode (listening, reading or speaking), then select from a series of highlighted activities that are listed under the different levels. You can learn over 1,000 words by playing games like bingo and concentration, and take part in comprehension quizzes and comic-strip conversations, using the record and play-back facility to check your delivery and accent. There are also word games to help with grammar and a Sound Start section where you can learn new words and check your pronunciation with the speech meter, which lights up to gauge your accuracy.

● A refresher course

If you already speak some French, but need to brush up on your vocabulary, *Ecoutez!* from EuroTalk might be for you. As the name suggests, the emphasis is on listening and understanding, rather than speaking, and the spoken French is delivered rapidly as it would be in real life.

There are two separate CD-ROMs, each with 10 lessons on different themes, ranging from telling the time and the days of the week, to the beach, careers and giving the right reply. Each lesson opens with an illustration, which forms the basis of a comprehension quiz. Your score is recorded each time you play, so it's easy to monitor your progress.

CONTACT POINTS

French for Everyone
Price: £19.99*
Mindscape
Tel: 01664 481 563
www.mindscape.com

Teaching-you French
Price: £9.99*
Focus Multimedia
Tel: 01889 570 156
www.focusmm.co.uk

Ecoutez!
Price: £19.99*
EuroTalk
Tel: 0800 018 8838
www.eurotalk.co.uk   *UK prices

Driving school

If you're learning to drive or simply want to brush up your driving skills, why not get behind the wheel of a driving tutorial program?

In the same way as pilots often learn to fly new aeroplanes in computer-operated flight simulators before they ever get in the real aircraft, so you can use the power of the PC to learn driving skills in the safety of your own home.

While CD-ROM driving tutorial programs are nowhere near as sophisticated as flight simulators, they can improve the skills of more experienced drivers and provide invaluable help for the student driver who is preparing for a driving test. Now that driving tests include a written element, the only way to learn the answers to all the questions is by serious study, followed by repeated testing. Driving tutorial programs help you do this in an interesting and effective way.

● Official packages

Among the best-known driving tutorials are *AA Pass First Time* from BTL Publishing, *Driving Test Success* from Focus Multimedia, and *Pass Your Driving Theory Test* from N-E Learning. All three set out to give you a thorough grounding in the essential skills and rules of the road. With the help of animations and videos of real driving situations, these discs are intended to help the beginner pass the driving test and the experienced driver to become a better driver. You'll also find a good deal of general information and questions to test your knowledge.

● First time lucky

AA Pass First Time covers all the official questions and answers for car and motorbike tests in one package. You can revise any of 14 main topics in any combination, so you focus on the areas which you think you are having most trouble with. Then you can create your own test bank of questions to review specific areas.

The program records and displays details of topics covered, along with the percentage of correct answers. This way you can get a feel for how good or bad you are to start with, then appreciate your improvement.

When you feel up to it, you can take a complete mock test under timed exam conditions. Additionally, the program provides advice on preparing for the theory and practical tests. As with most driving school CD-ROMs, a new edition is released each year incorporating the very latest amendments to the official tests and the Highway Code itself.

Having passed the test in real life, the CD-ROM continues to offer useful information, from economy tips for the road user to advice on buying second-hand vehicles.

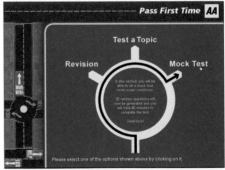

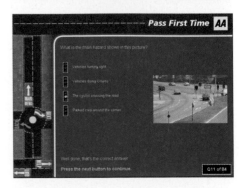

In AA Pass First Time you begin with categorized revision before moving on to the graded self-tests. Also included is a good collection of photo-based hazard and Highway Code examples prior to your final mock exam.

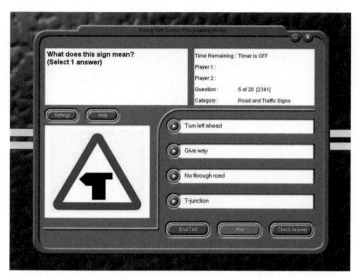

The questions in Driving Test Success are presented in multiple-choice format.

● Hazardous occupation

N-E Learning's *Pass Your Driving Theory Test* is a visually appealing Multimedia program which makes the most of its Flash-based interface. A built-in narrator will even read the questions aloud if you want.

Again this program covers motorcyling as well as cars, and adheres to the latest official test questions, being produced under licence from the Driving Standards Agency (DSA). During practice and at the end of mock theory tests, you are presented with full results and feedback so you can gauge how you are doing. The latest edition includes the official Hazard Perception video and mock test.

● Driving to success

Focus Multimedia's *Driving Test Success* CD-ROM aims to be a completely comprehensive guide to the questions you will encounter in the driving theory exam. It contains every question in the 'question bank' that the DSA uses to generate the real exams. It also covers both car and motorbike driving tests.

In Learning Mode, you get instant feedback on whether you've got the answer right, and there's a Hints button to help you if you're stumped. If you want some practice for the theory exam itself, you can switch to the program's Virtual Examination Mode. Based on the answers you give, the software identifies strengths and weaknesses so that you can

brush up in key areas later.

There are also extra questions that take you beyond what is strictly required in the driving theory exam: the Extra Signs section includes more than 80 questions on road signs, and the Observation and Common Mistakes sections provide another 80 safe-driving practice questions. The latter are based on the 80 video clips built into the software.

● What you learn

There's no doubt these CD-ROMs will help learners as they approach the driving test. They're no substitute, of course, for time spent driving a car, nor do they replace proper study of the full Highway Code. But what they do excel at is supplying a fresh and interactive way of improving and testing your driving knowledge.

Given the written element of the driving exam, taking lots of randomly generated tests is an effective way of making road sense stick in the mind. The video footage gives a feeling of the real world and sharpens drivers' observation skills. While the CD-ROMs are aimed at the learner driver, experienced motorists might well be surprised at how these videos can help brush up their skills, too.

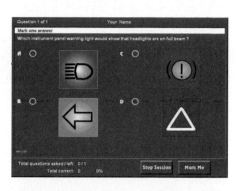

Knowing the road isn't enough – Pass Your Driving Theory Test ensures you know how your vehicle operates too.

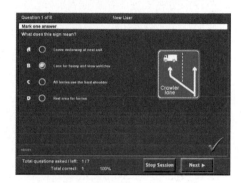

As you progress through your revision and self-testing, a tally is maintained of your correct answers. You can tell how you are doing from the percentage at the bottom.

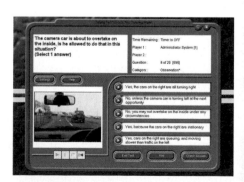

The video clips in the Observation section of Driving Test Success pose tricky questions to alert new drivers to hazards they won't be aware of.

Family health encyclopedias

Help yourself and your family to better health by using your computer and its Multimedia capabilities.

Your computer can not only help ensure you keep the family first aid box properly stocked, it will also show you what to do in the event of an emergency.

Modern-day pressures and emotional stresses conspire with the pollution of the cities in which many of us live to make it difficult for us to stay healthy. It could also be said that many of the foods we eat are bad for us and most of our favourite drinks do us little good either. But, with a little application and help, you can learn how to stay healthy and get fit by understanding how your body works and knowing what you can do to keep it working properly, or what to do if you fall ill.

● Fully booked

There are many medical reference books available, but these are often full of difficult medical terms and provide little practical, day-to-day information. A better alternative is to use the Multimedia power of your computer in the form of an electronic medical encyclopedia. As with books, these discs are not a substitute for expert advice – if in doubt, always contact your doctor.

A CD-ROM-based medical reference work will enable you to find the information you need instantly and efficiently, and cross-references all the information relevant to your query. Video demonstrations, animation and illustrations are used to show how to exercise correctly or perform life-saving first aid. On some of the discs, animation demonstrates how parts of your body work. The choice of which CD-ROM to go for will depend on the requirements of you and your family.

● Consult the BMA

To help empty your shelves of your existing medical reference works, there is Dorling Kindersley's *The BMA Family Health Encyclopedia*. It is full of authoritative, easy-to-understand information, with more than 750 illustrations, 200 photographs and 60 animations and videos – all that information on one CD-ROM certainly saves a lot of shelf space. It has full British

REASSURANCE

If you're the type of person who prefers not to know what your medical treatment might involve, you are probably not the ideal purchaser of a medical encyclopedia program. However, the clear and concise explanations, narration and video footage could reassure a worried patient about relatively minor and commonplace surgical procedures that offer a chance to return to good health.

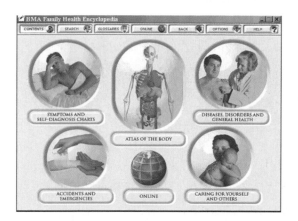

The BMA Family Health Encyclopedia *is an all-round user-friendly reference that helps you understand your body, the nature of diseases, treatments and what you can do to encourage health.*

The symptoms and self-diagnosis section is a useful diagnostic tool. If there is any doubt at all about the nature of your ailment, the message 'Call the doctor!' will be displayed in no uncertain terms.

Medical Association approval and manages to remain completely free of confusing jargon and complex medical terminology.

● Five sections

The encyclopedia itself is divided into five sections, comprising: symptoms and self-diagnosis charts; atlas of the body; diseases, disorders and general health; accidents and emergencies; and caring for yourself and others.

You can also access Dorling Kindersley's Health Club Web site from within the encyclopedia, where there are articles on health-related topics ranging from information on training gear to diets and healthy recipes. The symptoms and diagnosis section contains 99 easy-to-follow charts setting out a series of questions to which you answer Yes or No. The diagnosis given depends on these answers, and the program will then alert you if you need to make an appointment to see your family doctor.

The diseases, disorders and general health section contains 650 straightforward articles, all cross-referenced and thematically presented to assist diagnosis and accompanied by explanations of common medical tests and treatments.

● First Aid

If you want more specialist first aid advice, *Interactive First Aid* is published in collaboration with St John's Ambulance. This could be the most important CD-ROM you ever buy, because not only is it an excellent reference tool, it is also an invaluable teacher, helping you to acquire the knowledge and skills to practise first aid in the real world.

The CD-ROM has four chapters: first principles; conditions; first aid in action; and the first aid kit. It takes you through assessing an accident scene, making it safe, getting help, giving aid to casualties, recognizing symptoms, knowing what treatment to give and spotting danger signs. You can then test your knowledge on five accident scenes.

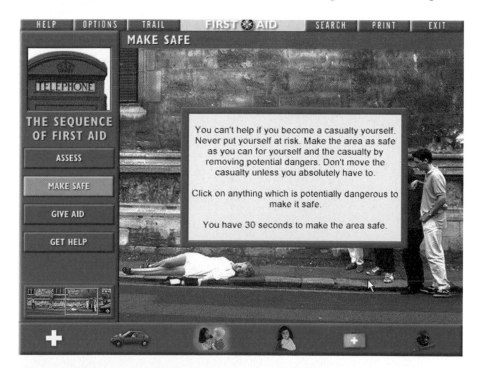

This isn't a real incident, but part of the **Interactive First Aid** *CD-ROM published in collaboration with St John's Ambulance. The CD-ROM allows you to put everything you learn from the program into practice in situations such as the one shown here. This knowledge could result in you making a big difference at a real accident scene.*

CONTACT POINTS

DK's The BMA Family Health Encyclopedia
Price: £9.99*
GSP
Tel: 01480 496 666
www.gsp.cc

Interactive First Aid
Price: £9.99*
Focus Multimedia
Tel: 01889 570 156
www.focusmm.co.uk

*UK prices

Computers in the movies

With increasingly sophisticated computer techniques now being used in films, it is becoming more difficult to tell fact from fiction.

In 1897, Englishman R.W. Paul created the first-ever movie special effect. His work, entitled *The Railway Collision*, featured a train crash which was faked by filming model trains in a miniature landscape.

Simple though it sounds, the use of physical models and cinematic sleight of hand was the norm for most special effects until very recently. But, with the advent of computers and computer-generated images (CGIs), film-makers now have almost unlimited scope in the types of 'special fx' they can create and what they can show.

Despite some early special-effects innovations, such as those featured in *King Kong* (1933), little progress was made until the 1960s, by which time director Stanley Kubrick had made the critically acclaimed *2001: A Space Odyssey*. This was the first film to use motion-controlled cameras connected to a computer. These cameras allowed for the long

Godzilla stalks the streets in the 1998 movie of the same name. In this film the effects were the star.

TRICK OF THE LIGHT

The methods might change, but some tricks of special-effects technicians remain the same: a good way to make an effect look real is to show as little of it as possible and let the audience's imagination fill in the details. In *Jurassic Park*, for example, there's actually less than 10 minutes of computer-generated dinosaur footage, but by quickly cutting back and forth, as well as setting much of the dinosaur action in the dark, a convincing illusion was created.

panning shots that were especially useful in filming the model spacecraft used in the movie. The film was the training ground for many technicians who would then go on to work on the legendary feature film *Star Wars*.

George Lucas's original *Star Wars* trilogy used every special-effects trick available, improving on all of them in the process. The most important of these tricks was the work done with computer-controlled cameras.

● A new force in filming

By programming a computer with an exact series of movements, it became possible to move the cameras in exactly the same way time after time, and so film the same sequence identically over and over again.

Dreams of a full-length feature film starring entirely digital actors became a reality for the first time in 2001 with the release of **Final Fantasy (The Spirits Within).**

This allowed different elements, such as spaceships, backdrops and explosions, to be captured one at a time, so that when they were combined, a single, seamless image could be created.

However, this was only the beginning and George Lucas's Industrial Light & Magic (ILM) special effects company would go on to weave even more extravagant computerized magic. *The Last Starfighter*, made in 1984, was

The widely publicized Star Wars Special Edition featured an entirely new CGI scene with Jabba the Hutt (right). Part of the process involved the creation of a virtual wireframe model (left) that was added to old footage of Harrison Ford. The model was then rendered.

one of the first films to make wide use of CGIs (computer-generated images). This movie used CGIs in a way that is essentially the same as is used today. First, a computer-generated wireframe model of the intended effect, for example a spaceship or a dinosaur, is created. This looks something like a model made out of chicken wire and is used to experiment with the movements and positioning of the effect on screen.

© 20th Century Fox

Recent years have seen an explosion in the number of computer-animated films created for children, such as Ice Age with its 3D cartoon-like animal characters.

● Extra texture

When the technician is satisfied with the wireframe, textures are introduced so that it appears solid, and additional layers of lighting and atmospheric effects are then added. Once a scene is set up, it then has to be rendered. This process takes a long time and requires a lot of expensive computers with massive processing power. At the end you are left with a single frame of movie footage.

The use of CGI signalled the giant leap from computers being just another aid to traditional techniques, to their being a means of generating special effects on their own. Soon 'effects-only' movies were being hyped at the cinemas, with the main attraction being the quality of the

special effects and the loud, explosive soundtracks. It's difficult to imagine recent hits such as *Godzilla* or *Armageddon* attracting as much public interest without their state-of-the-art effects.

● CGI judgement day

In 1991, *Terminator 2: Judgement Day (T2)* featured another computer breakthrough (also from ILM) in which audiences were able to see the evil T-1000 Terminator change its shape by flowing like mercury from one form into another. Quite simply, a computer had created the world's first virtual actor, existing nowhere but on the computer and on film. The effect was limited by the technology of the time, but led to much speculation that future films might see an entirely computer-generated cast. Ten years later, convincing human characters created by CGI became a reality with *Final Fantasy (The Spirits Within)*, prompting speculation that one day it may be possible to bring back famous faces from the past to a new virtual life on-screen.

The techniques first seen in *T2* were later refined by ILM in 1993's *Jurassic Park* and its two sequels. For the movie industry, though, the biggest revelation was in monetary terms: it's cheaper to use CGI than traditional model work. Even a film as innovative as *Jurassic Park* cost less than $100 million to make, compared to the $200 million spent on Kevin Costner's *Waterworld*, which used

mostly model shots and full-size sets. Not surprisingly many types of film now use this new technology, particularly animated movies.

Disney's entirely computer-created *Toy Story* and *A Bug's Life* were both enormous hits. By the time *Toy Story 2* appeared, scores of other CGI animated films for children were in production, including *Dinosaur, Monsters Inc* and the Oscar-winning *Shrek*. Computer animation mixed with live action has also been popular in movies such as *Spy Kids*, *Stuart Little* and *Scooby-Doo*.

CGI has now become a standard feature of action movies, from *Lord of the Rings* to *Starship Troopers*, and *Hollow Man* to *Spider-Man*. There's certainly no going back to expensive hand-built models.

This shot of a Brachiosaurus was one of the least convincing computer animations from Jurassic Park – largely because it was shot in strong daylight.

Tracing your family tree

Everyone is interested in where they came from and who their ancestors were, but tracing your family tree can be a long and complicated process. Your PC can be the perfect research assistant.

The beauty of using your PC to research your family history is that, with most programs, when you add new information to the database, the software takes care of redrawing the family tree for you.

Genealogy, the study of ancestry and family histories, holds a fascination for all of us, but tracing your roots can prove a frustrating task. Your PC can help to take the hard work out of searching and collating family facts and will present them in a clear format so you can see how your family has changed over the generations.

A whole range of family tree programs offer the computer-based genealogist a variety of functions and features. Some software offers a suite of programs including graphics and Internet software, whereas others are useful for creating the on-screen equivalent of a family album.

Here we've taken a close look at GSP's *Family Tree v3* and Focus Multimedia's *Create your Family Tree with 'The Master Genealogist'*.

● Help with your search
If you are new to genealogy, you need a straightforward program that offers some guidance on doing your research and a well-ordered framework for storing the data you gather on individual family members.

Family Tree does both of these. An extensive help section lists useful contacts and sources of genealogical information and includes a printable form with standard questions that you can use as a basis for your investigations and interviews.

There are also hints on how to collect and record information,

including keeping a note of your sources and taking copies of documents. A research facility acts as a personal memo, enabling you to keep track of where you are with your research on each individual, which sources you've checked and what you still have to do.

Once you've entered your data into individual records for each family member, you can create your family tree. If you have photographs, these can be attached to the records and displayed as part of the tree. A variety of backgrounds, fonts and borders can then be selected to create an historic-looking document, which can be printed out for the family archive or given to other relations.

● Photo albums
One real bonus of using your PC to help collate your family tree is that you can store more than basic facts. It's especially easy and useful to set up a computer scrapbook to store photographs of people at various ages, and much more besides.

People's jobs or achievements can personalize the record, as can voice recordings or scanned documents such as birth and marriage certificates, award and

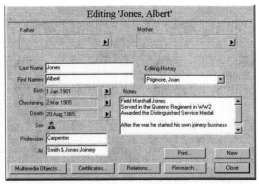

Genealogical programs like Family Tree make it easy to record information on your relatives. A standard form (above) allows you to enter details and make notes.

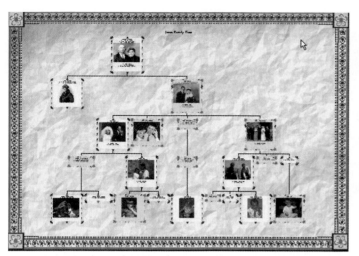

Keep an on-screen family album, such as this one from Family Tree, to tell the story of your family throughout the years.

Create Your Family Tree *allows you to enter extensive information on each individual so you can build up an interesting chronology of their life.*

exam certificates, favourite drawings or paintings and written memories. These will preserve the character of your family for generations to come. *Family Tree* includes a photo album as part of the program. This automatically arranges the photos in your tree into chronological order to create a Multimedia family album.

● Collating information

A genealogy program comes into its own once you have a growing mountain of information. It is pointless collecting all this information if it's impossible to make any sense of it. *Create your Family Tree* is less about printing out a decorative family tree or keeping a photo album, and more about enabling in-depth research.

Designed by professional genealogists, historians and librarians to encourage good research and documentation methods, it is an impressive research tool that allows you to record all the data you discover on every family member, including alternative dates, names, spellings, known and even suspected information about them.

This is a complex program, with a 387-page reference manual, but the basics are simple enough. All the information known on each person is entered on that individual's Person View. From here you can navigate from one person to another, or to the original entry screen with the full details of an entry, by double-clicking on that entry. Pictures and documents can also be attached.

● Web sites

The Internet has become an increasingly vital link in the chain of genealogy resources. Some programs have direct links to popular UK genealogy Web sites such as www.genealogy.co.uk, which gives details of archives and libraries for England, Scotland and Wales and surname lists by county.

The Mormons' Family Search site (www.familysearch.org) logs a massive 600 million names which church members have been collecting for decades from all known genealogical records. You simply type in as much information as you have available in the way of names, and the site brings up its results.

CONTACT POINTS

Family Tree v3
Price: £19.99*
GSP
Tel: 01480 496 666
www.gsp.cc

Create Your Family Tree with 'The Master Genealogist' Silver UK Edition
Price: £9.99*
Focus Multimedia
Tel: 01889 570 156
www.focusmm.co.uk

*UK prices

PC TIPS

To get the most out of your family tree computer program, you will probably want to store family photos along with the information. One way to get these pictures into your computer is to find a local computer bureau, printer or even a local library that offers a scanning service – you give them your pictures and they'll transfer them to disk for you. This may prove expensive, however, if you want to do this often. Another option is to invest in a basic scanner. This device scans your photos into your computer as images for you to print and store.

You can keep a simple text-based family tree, but adding photographs can help to give a fuller picture of your family's life in years gone by. Ensure that your information, including picture captions, is accurate, or your mistakes could go down in history.

Platform games

For pure fun and enjoyment, it's hard to beat the colourful and challenging world of the platform game.

Throughout computer history, some of the most popular games have been based on one simple action: not shooting or punching, but simply jumping. Programs that feature such action are known as platform games and have been around almost as long as computer games themselves.

Despite their apparent simplicity, such games have proved that jumping skills have just as much entertainment value in the computer's virtual reality world as they do on the athletics field.

● A slow start

In the early days, platform games used to be static, non-scrolling affairs. The ultimate goal might simply be to get across to the other side of the screen, but it often involved collecting a few objects along the way.

To add extra jeopardy to the proceedings, the screen was made up of several free-standing platforms, often no more sophisticated than flat horizontal lines. These were placed in increasingly awkward positions, so

you had to use your expertise to judge when to jump from one to another. Usually, monsters would move around the area through which you had to jump, putting you under extra pressure to get your timing exactly right, while accurately judging the distance and height you had to leap.

● Into a third dimension

Early home computer titles, such as *Manic Miner* and *Jet Set Willy*, gave way to more skill-based (as opposed to purely reflex-based) titles such as *Super Mario Bros*. The platform game continued to evolve and change but the basic concept remained: to get from one end of a game world to the other without falling off a platform or getting killed by the ferocious monsters.

Up to that point, all platform games were two-dimensional. However, the increasing popularity of high-powered PCs as game machines through the 1990s changed

Duke Nukem: Manhattan Project *(above) and the forthcoming* Rayman 3 *(top) hail the return of classic platformers but this time with 3D-enhanced graphics.*

all this. Rapid improvements in graphics hardware and the Windows operating system itself began to put real-time 3D character interaction at the forefront of games development.

The classic 2D 'platformer' was largely replaced by 'action/adventure' games such as *Quake* and *Unreal* in which you effectively run around a platform-style environment in 3D, seen from a first-person perspective. But the tide is changing yet again with the arrival of **superconsoles** and a renewed interest in gameplay over graphics. A good example is *Duke Nukem: Manhattan Project*, where the archetypal first-person 3D shoot-'em-up has been reborn as a 2D scrolling platform game, albeit with superb graphics.

At the same time, many best-selling titles were followed up with 3D sequels, such as *Earthworm Jim 3D*,

WHAT IT MEANS

SUPERCONSOLES

Just as the PC has evolved and improved over the years, so too have video-game machines – to the point where their graphical power can match even a top-of-the-range PC. The previous market leaders in games consoles, such as the Nintendo64 and Sony PlayStation, have now given way to a new group, collectively known as superconsoles, which includes Nintendo's GameCube, the PlayStation 2, and now also the Xbox from Microsoft. Increasingly, games originally written for consoles are reprogrammed to run on PCs.

challenges, environments to explore, traps to avoid and secrets to be found, in true platform tradition.

These new trends may signify that the games market is turning full circle, with platform-style games set to dominate once more in the future.

Tony Hawk's Pro Skater 3 is the ultimate lifestyle platform game, full of challenges and secret rooms.

Movie tie-ins abound in the world of platform games, ably demonstrated by Harry Potter and the Philosopher's Stone (above) and the cartoon web-slinger Spider-man: The Movie (left).

while new ones were given the 3D treatment from the start, for example those in the *Croc* series, such as *Croc 2*. The popular console platformer *Rayman* is also due a 3D-enhanced return to the PC in *Rayman 3: Hoodlum Havoc*.

● Character building

The key to most platform games is, of course, an interest in the central character, whether that be the aforementioned Duke or *Tomb Raider*'s Lara Croft. For this reason, platform-style games have always

Even a single-toothed baby crocodile can save the world (or his friends, the Gobbos at least). Platform hero Croc follows in a long line of unlikely main characters, from blue hedgehogs to Italian plumbers.

been the obvious choice for movie tie-ins. Just about every action character from James Bond to Robocop and the Terminator, and even the creatures from Aliens and Predator, have enjoyed platform game success.

Following on from the likes of the Batman franchise is *Spider-man: The Movie*, obviously created to tie in with the movie as well as the long-running comic series. Here you get to battle the Goblin and swing between skyscrapers in a 3D-enriched arena.

Another popular movie-to-game conversion has been *Harry Potter and the Philosopher's Stone*, in which you explore Hogwarts school, solve puzzles, interact with other characters and inevitably play Quidditch. In a nice design touch, subtle changes occur to the environment as you play, so don't expect a secret passage to stay in the same place for long!

● New challenges

Between action-adventure and kids' stuff, a gulf has opened for a new style of game. Many of these games are theme-based, borrowing from other genres such as puzzles and sport.

Tony Hawk's Pro Skater 3 typifies this new gaming approach. Apart from letting you perform tricks, this skateboard title isn't quite the sport or racing game you might expect. Instead, it presents you with a set of

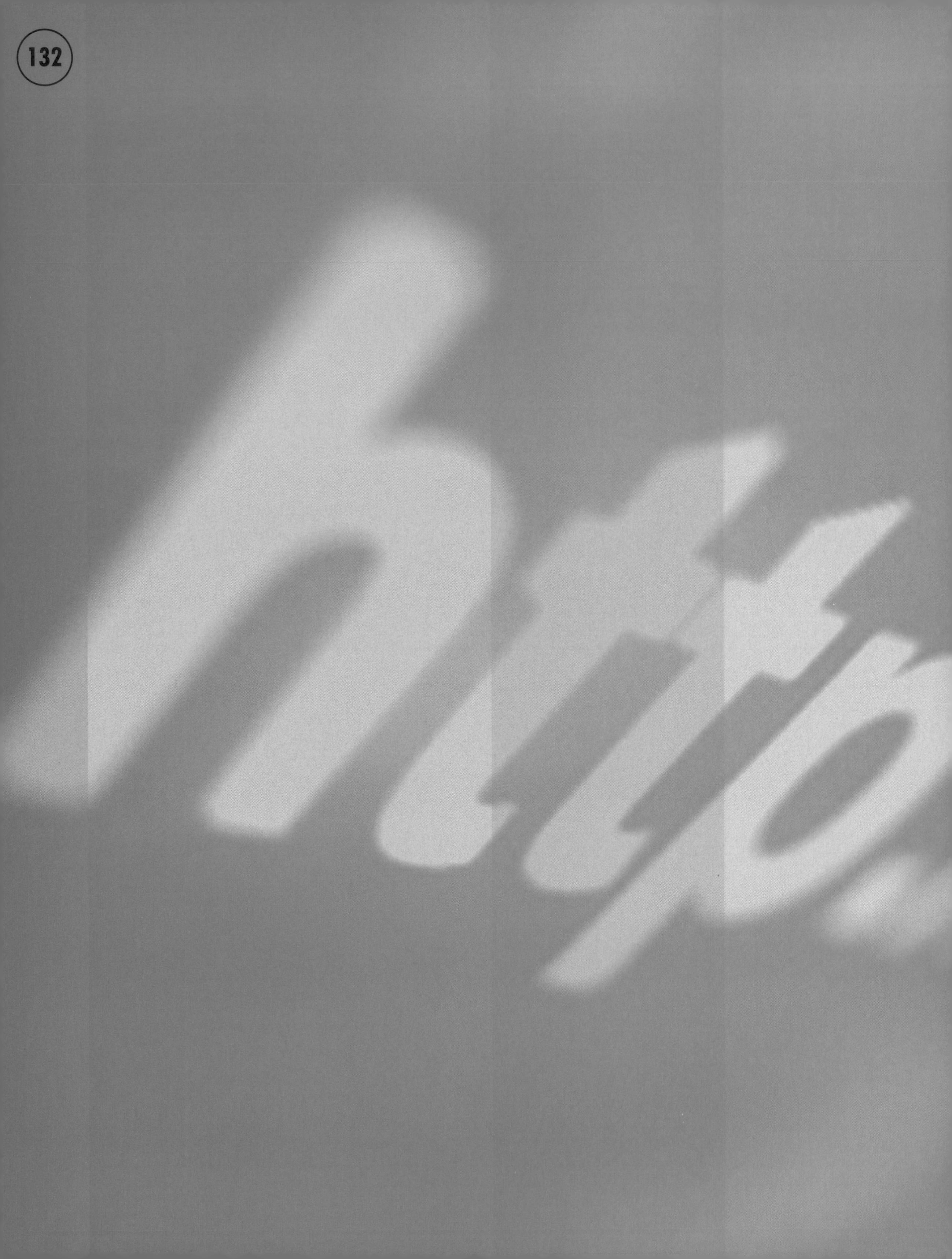

The Internet

Easy Web browsing

There is a place for everything and almost everything has a place on the Internet. No matter how diverse your interests, they will be catered for. We show you where to look.

The single reason for the Internet becoming so popular is the World Wide Web; this is a collection of millions of pages of fun, programs and information stored on computers all around the world. Before the Web came along, the Internet was hard to use and only experts really gained much value from it.

With the World Wide Web (often abbreviated to www), the Internet became

Your browser helps you find what you want from the vast mass of information on the Internet. You can use your browser to find Web sites you already know or for making general searches.

that are used to create a Web page and displays the text and images in the intended format. Moving around Web pages and using hyperlinks is called browsing, or sometimes 'surfing'. However, before you can start browsing the pages on the Web, you need to get connected to the Internet and sign up with an Internet service provider (see Stage 1, pages 136–139).

● Browser connection
When you start your Web browser, it checks to see if you are already connected to the Internet. If you are not, it will start the software that dials up and connects you – you'll see a dialog box that asks you to confirm that you want to connect. Click on the Connect button and you'll hear your modem dial out.

Once it establishes a connection with your Internet service provider, you'll be able to start browsing. There are two main types of browser available – Microsoft's Internet Explorer (which comes with Windows XP) and Netscape's Communicator/Navigator. One of them will also be supplied by a user's ISP when it sends the start-up software needed for a Web connection. Although there are differences between the two, they will both allow you to move around the Web, viewing pages, images, video and animation.

WHAT IT MEANS

HTML

Almost all Web pagea are created using a language called hypertext mark-up language, or HTML, which defines the way text is displayed. HTML is used for all parts of a Web page, from bold text to hyperlinks. For example, the code <b> will display text in bold. Your browser displays Web pages without showing the HTML code.

as easy to use as Windows itself. You can just point and click your way from page to page across the world. Each Web page can contain text, images, sound, video clips and animation – just like a Multimedia CD-ROM.

● Browsing around
To view a page you need to use a program called a Web browser. This converts the special HTML codes

Changing your start-up Web page

After a while, you might notice that the site at which your Web browser starts isn't very interesting. Save time and money by choosing your own favourite site as your start-up Web address.

EACH TIME you start your Web browser, it will automatically display the initial welcome page from the same Web site – usually one created by the Web browser maker, or your ISP. Many ISPs have made their home pages into gateways – 'portals' – to the Web that offer news and services, together with links to a wealth of selected content. If you use such an ISP you may well be happy to stick with it as your home page.

● **Saving money**

However, if you have to wait for a relatively uninteresting page to load, you are wasting both time and money. In this case it might be worth changing your home page. There is a significant financial benefit to cutting down on waiting time. For example, if your family starts the browser three times a day on average, and this welcome page takes 30 seconds to load, you are wasting 630 seconds per week. That's 546 minutes a year, at a cost of around £22 at peak rates. You can easily change the first page to a favourite one or leave it blank for a faster start-up.

Microsoft Internet Explorer

The Internet Explorer start-up page is the Microsoft Network, which contains all sorts of links to news and features. But it might not be the right mix for you.

To change the Internet Explorer start-up page, go to the Tools menu and select Internet Options. Click the General tab if that page is not already on screen. Select the current Web address under Home page and type in the new one, such as www.football365.co.uk. Click OK to save the changes and restart the browser. For a blank page, just click the Use Blank button.

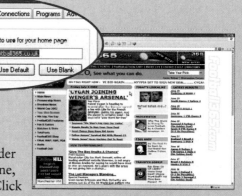

If you can't get enough of football, try making your home page an up-to-the minute soccer site like Football365 (www.football365.co.uk).

Netscape Communicator/Navigator

Netscape's opening page has links to all kinds of news and services – perhaps too many to make it an ideal home page.

To change your start-up page in Netscape Communicator or Navigator, choose Preferences from the Edit menu. In the Home Page box select the currently displayed address and type in the new one. Click OK and then restart the browser for the changes to take effect. If you prefer a blank page, simply click the Blank page option at the top of the page.

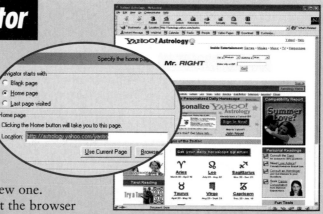

It might be more fun to have your favourite horoscope page displayed each time you log on. Try http://astrology.yahoo.com/yastro for a daily forecast.

Searching for information

The best way to navigate the millions of sites on the World Wide Web is to use a search engine. Just enter your enquiry and the search engine will give you a list of sites that match it.

IF YOU ALREADY know where you want to go on the Internet and you have the address of the Web site, then you can type it directly into your browser. To find a site to answer a particular question, or to find information on a special subject, you first need to find the address of a site that holds the answer. Search engines are Web sites dedicated to finding addresses for practically any query imaginable.

Search engines are rather like huge telephone directories. You enter key words instead of flicking through pages and the search engine responds with addresses instead of telephone numbers. For example, if you want to find out about bee-keeping in New York, you could type in the search words 'bee-keeping' and 'New York' to see if the search engine has any Web pages that contain these terms. If there are any matches, or 'hits', you will see a summary of the contents of the Web page and a hyperlink so you can jump directly to the page.

● **Selecting a search engine**
There are several search engines that are worth using to find information. One is Yahoo! – one of the most comprehensive search engines and certainly one of the best known. Yahoo! organizes information into categories that make it easier to find a Web site. Yell is provided by the Yellow Pages directory in the UK and is a good choice if you want UK Web sites. Google is comprehensive and provides specialized advanced search features, while AltaVista is one of the most powerful and comprehensive search engines available. See pages 138–141 for further details on searching the Web.

HOW A SEARCH ENGINE WORKS

A search engine tries to index the text contained in every single page on the World Wide Web. Since there are millions of Web pages and many change almost every day, this is no mean feat. Some search engines try to provide the most exhaustive directory of Web pages, while others provide reviews to help you choose the best sites to visit. Try several of the Web search engines listed in the Sites To Visit box on the opposite page to see which works best for you.

When researching a work or school project, you don't need to know the exact address of any sites. Entering specific keywords such as 'biology frog lifespan' will usually provide some suggested sites to visit.

ADDRESSES ON THE WORLD WIDE WEB

Every page on the Web has a unique address. Wherever you are in the world, just typing the address into your browser takes you directly to it. In computer jargon, this address is called the Uniform Resource Locator or URL.

Often a URL looks something like: www.disney.com. The 'www' part signifies that you are looking for a Web page; the second part shows the name of the Web site (Disney); and the third part identifies the type of Web site (.com is a commercial site). To say the URL aloud, read it as 'w-w-w-dot-disney-dot-com'.

To view this page, just type the address into your browser's URL line. When you press the [Enter] key, your browser goes direct to the Disney Web site. When the first page has finished loading, you can see individual pages on the site by clicking on the links on the page (often marked in blue).

As you click on these links, look to see what happens to the URL line: it changes to show another URL. The first part looks the same but the whole URL is longer and refers to other pages on the Disney site.

Using Yahoo! to find a Web site

You can find virtually anything on the World Wide Web – if you know where to go. Let's look for a specific car – the MG ZS, with the help of Yahoo!

1 Enter the Yahoo! URL (www.yahoo.com) into your Web browser to display its welcome page (right). It may not look very exciting, but it might soon become a favourite port of call. You can type search words (sometimes called keywords) into the text box or use the ready-made categories (inset) to narrow down your search. You can enter just one keyword or a specific query that includes several.

2 Clicking on Recreation & Sports from Yahoo's Web Site Directory takes us to this screen, which you can scroll down using your mouse to reveal the next possible choices, listed alphabetically. As we are looking for information about cars, we select the Automotive category.

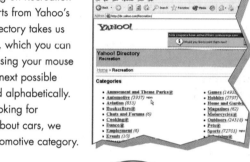

3 A further list of options appears. We know the MG was a British car, so this category will be our next choice. Click once on the link to access the information under British cars.

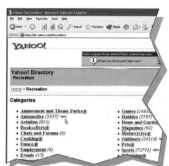

4 As you can see, searching on the Internet with a search engine is like following a trail of clues. This not only makes it easy to find what you want, it also makes it a lot more fun. Here are the options which are listed under British Cars. Now select the MG category.

5 Now a list of the Web sites relating to MG cars appears. Scrolling down the page brings up a site which specializes in MG Rovers. Clicking on the title of the site takes you straight there, with no need to type in the address. Then it's a matter of looking around the pages of the site by clicking on links to find the information you need (inset).

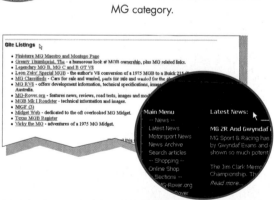

6 One of the exciting things about looking for something on the Internet is the huge amount of information that is available. There were many distractions on the way to the MG Rover page we wanted to look at, so we could easily have wandered off track and investigated the MG road tests or read up on recent motorsport news.

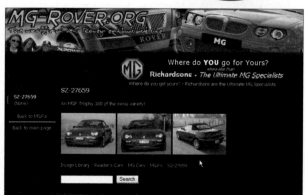

Effective Web searching

Finding precisely what you want on the ever-expanding World Wide Web isn't easy. But if you use one of the many search engines available, you'll soon be able to locate a needle in a haystack.

The more you use the Web, the more you'll become aware that you need help to get to what you want. It's okay if you know the full addresses, or URLs, of the sites you want to visit; you just type them into your Web browser. However, while it's possible to limit yourself to the few trusty sites you know, you would be ignoring the true power of the Web if you did not cast your net wider.

For Web browsing where you don't know the address but you have a good idea of the type of information you want, you need to use a search engine. These are powerful Internet sites that exist purely to help you find other sites based on a few key words.

A search engine has two parts. The first, which you don't see, continuously trawls through millions of Web pages and creates a huge index of the words contained in them. The second is the Web page, which you use to search the index that's been created by the first part. It reports back with the relevant Web addresses, and all you do is click on the list of links to go to the Web site.

● **Search engine choices**
The search engines on the Web can be divided into two broad categories: those organized by subject or topic, and those which use text searches.

Yahoo! (www.yahoo.co.uk) is a good example of the first type. When you visit the site, you can click through a series of subject headings to see more specific categories (see page 137). With this type of site, you needn't type anything at all – just search, point and click.

With UKPlus, you need only point and click your way through a series of subject categories to find a list of Web sites you may want to visit.

The weakness inherent in this type of searching, however, is that it can take a lot of clicking and loading of successive Web pages to find sites you are interested in. If you are looking for very specific information, it's better to take advantage of the text searches available.

● Text-based searches

AltaVista (www.altavista.com) is one of the most popular text-based search engines. When the Web page loads you will see a simple text box into which you can type anything you like. When you press the Search button, AltaVista searches its index for the words you have typed.

Try the search engine and you will find that the more general the words that you type – for example, 'dinosaur' or 'fishing' – the longer the list of sites it finds. It will present them in groups of 20 sites at a time, and you will have to check through the descriptions, or even visit the sites themselves, to see if any contain the information you want.

For this reason, it's better to be as specific as possible with your search. Searching for 'triceratops', for instance, will yield fewer pages than searching for 'dinosaur'. In fact, the key to getting to relevant sites quickly (minimizing time and costs) is to exploit the way in which text-based search engines work.

There are special characters and phrases you can use to improve your search. While they might seem a little daunting at first sight, they are fast and extremely powerful once you know how to get the most out of them.

● Special commands

Search engines use many tricks, but among the more powerful are those known as 'Boolean operators'. The name is a mathematical phrase for what are simply logical words that can be used to define your search. The four most commonly used operators are AND, OR, NOT and NEAR.

● Using the operators

These operators work just as they sound. For example, you would type 'fishing AND bass' to locate Web pages which feature both (thereby avoiding general fishing pages and those that cover bass guitars).

The other operators are just as useful. For instance, the OR operator works in the opposite way to AND. Thus you might search for 'Mercedes OR Porsche OR Jaguar' to find Web pages that contain information on any of these makes of car. Note, however, that you will also locate pages about the jaguar wild cat, too.

The NOT operator is used if you want to exclude a subject. This is very useful if the word you are searching for has more than one meaning. For example, 'windows NOT computer' is a good way to find pages about window-panes rather than Microsoft Windows.

WHAT IT MEANS

SYNTAX

This refers to the grammatical structure of a search. Just like words in plain English, the order of commands in a search is important; it must be in a form the computer can understand.

The last of the four most common operators is NEAR, which is less frequently used than the other three. It can be useful if you are not sure how to describe the subject you are looking at, but can think of some specific words a page of interest should contain.

For example, 'ant NEAR nest NEAR society' could be a useful way to search for a scientific piece about ants if you didn't know that the study of ants is called myrmecology.

● Other text functions

The special text functions are just as easy to use. These are function words that work using a special syntax. They always end in a colon (:), followed by the word or phrase for which you are searching.

For example, 'anchor:boat' will search for pages that contain the word 'boat' in a link (or anchor, as links are known in AltaVista).

Other function words include 'domain' (for specific domain

Google is one example of a text-based search engine; if you type in a word or phrase, it will produce a list of all the sites it has found that contain the text.

names such as .org or .uk) and 'image' (useful for locating pictures with specific words in their names).

There are other function words that you will find detailed on the search engines' help pages.

● Fine-tuning your searches

With these simple additions to your text searches you will be able to narrow the field considerably. This means that you're less likely to be confronted by hundreds of Web pages – any one of which may include the information you want, but most of which will be a waste of time – thus making your search a great deal easier.

Using different search engines

To illustrate how difficult a specific search can be, we'll try to find three of Steven Spielberg's films, using Lycos and Yahoo!

SEARCH ENGINES such as Alta Vista and Lycos can turn up thousands of pages, however directory-based search engines, such as Yahoo!, pre-select certain sites. We show how either approach can get what you want – in this case, three films made by Steven Spielberg. Just typing in 'Steven Spielberg' isn't going to be much use here, as it will turn up literally thousands of Web pages. We'll look for the information using two different search engines. Lycos will search the Web and report back with as many sites as it can find containing your search term. Yahoo!, on the other hand, uses human staff to select the sites it lists for you. This can cut out a lot of rubbish and can sometimes be a quicker way to search.

1 Go to the Lycos search engine by typing 'www.lycos.co.uk' in your browser's URL line. Select Worldwide to search the whole Web rather than just UK sites. Then type in 'Steven Spielberg' in the Search for: box and click on the Go Get It! button.

2 Lycos finds well over 500,000 results. The information we want is in there somewhere, but it could take a long time to find it.

3 We need to refine our search. Type in Spielberg's name again, but now followed by three of his films separated by the ampersand (&) symbol – which is short for the Boolean operator AND. This should come up with sites listing Spielberg's films.

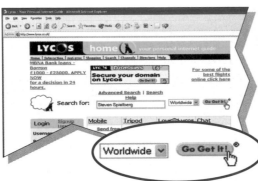

4 Now five Web sites are returned. Looking over the results, it looks like the interactive list of directors and producers could be the site we want. Clicking on it takes us to the site, where we find a biography of Spielberg, including information on the three films we are looking for.

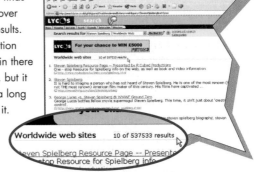

5 Now let's try Yahoo! (www.yahoo.com or www.yahoo.co.uk). We don't need to type anything in the Search box at first; instead, click on the Movies link in the Entertainment category.

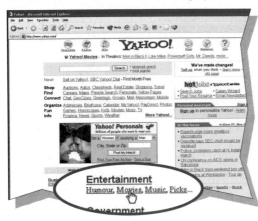

6 This brings up a number of movie-related sub-categories. Now we can refine our search. Type in the director's name in the Search box, then select the this category only option on the right. Now click on the Search button.

7 This brings up a list of sites specifically dealing with Spielberg's work. Very quickly we find a number of sites that contain the information we want.

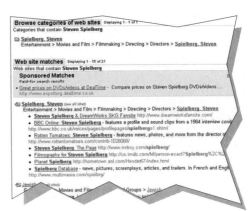

Searching for pictures, links and newsgroups

Sometimes you will want to search for things other than specific words used in the text of a Web page. This is where special text search functions come in.

BY USING the special text search functions in your searches you will be able to find items that a Web search would normally miss. For example, you can find pictures and links – both of which are parts of a Web page that a search engine would not normally look in. When you try these more advanced searches, you'll soon find search engines have strengths and weaknesses. Some are better suited to certain types of search than others. For example, Google has the facility to search the vast collection of newsgroup postings, whereas AltaVista allows you to look for words within links on a page. It's worth exploring the different areas of each search engine to see the full range of search facilities that are available. Look for Advanced Search or Help links on the home page of the search engines you visit to find out more.

1 To search Google for Usenet sites, first select the Groups option from the top row of boxes.

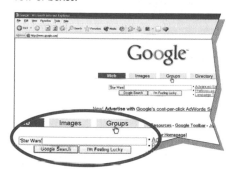

2 Now type in the subject and click on Google Search. We're looking for Star Wars, and we've enclosed the phrase in quotation marks to make sure that Google looks only for the two words next to each other.

3 Google then lists the matches it finds. Click on any one to see the individual message. Here someone is trying to sell their duplicate Star Wars collectibles.

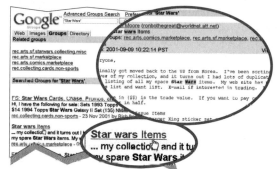

4 Visit AltaVista (www.altavista.com) and you can search for text within the links on a page. To do this, you need to type the command 'anchor:' before the word. Here we're looking for links that contain the word 'dinosaur'.

5 The matches are mostly dinosaur pages, all of which seem pretty interesting.

6 Most search engines have a specific page for searching for images – for example, AltaVista has an Images link at the top of the home page. Click this and you can specify a search term and the type of image you're looking for on the next page. The results page shows images with your search term in their links – click one to see it full size.

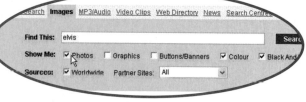

| 22492.jpg | eMs-sm.jpg | 22703.jpg |
| 369x500 28 KB | 321x307 70 KB | 330x400 25 KB |

METASEARCHING

Whether you're using a 'classic' search engine or a directory-style site, it can't possibly report all the pages that might be relevant. And, since each search engine uses its own technology and tricks, they will not all be equally accurate or comprehensive. If you want to do a really thorough search and cover all the bases, you might consider using what is called 'metasearch' software. These programs do not search the Web themselves, but take your query and get a number of different search engines to do it. The results can be impressively thorough.

Downloading software

The Internet is not only a great resource for information and entertainment, it also allows you to copy – or download – new programs and other useful software directly onto your computer.

The World Wide Web can be seen as a giant warehouse containing computer programs, text, photographs, video graphics and sound – all of which can be downloaded onto your home computer.

The Internet contains information on almost every subject, but it also has files that store programs, games, video footage, images and sounds. These files are stored on computers that are linked to the Internet, but you can copy a file onto your hard disk in order to use it. This process, called downloading, means that you can access new information or try out new programs quickly and cheaply.

Many Web pages have links that lead to a downloadable file, rather than to another Web page. If you click on one of these download links, your Web browser will automatically start to copy the file onto your computer's hard disk.

● **What you can download**

There is a wide range of different types of software that you can download and use at home. For example, many of the large software companies have trial versions of new or popular software for you to download and use before deciding whether to buy the full program.

There are demonstration versions of games that work for a few days or have a limited number of levels. New Internet technologies usually require new software and this is often available to download free of charge – for example, the QuickTime MoviePlayer Software, which allows you to run small video sequences on your PC. If you want to view 3D worlds or listen to music over the

Internet, you will need to add software to your Web browser to allow it to use this feature. This software – called a plug-in – is made available as the new technologies are developed and can be downloaded free to keep your Web browser up to date.

WHAT IT MEANS

PLUG-IN

A plug-in is a piece of software that extends the functions of a Web browser. Plug-ins are sometimes required for new Multimedia features in Web sites, such as video, audio, 3D graphics and animation. Plug-ins are usually supplied free and install automatically.

The Internet also allows you to download the latest drivers for graphics hardware and modems; if you have a problem with a software program, you can often find and download a special program, called a patch, that fixes the fault.

If you want new software, there are thousands of shareware programs to download. If you like a program and use it regularly, you pay a registration fee to the program developer. Shareware programs include drawing and painting programs, word processors and business tools.

● Find fantastic fonts

If you want to add new fonts (typefaces) to your computer or enhance a presentation with exciting graphic images, look on the Internet. There are thousands of different downloadable fonts created by professional designers – some are free and others offer a free trial period.

Download the QuickTime software (www.apple.com/ quicktime) and you will be able to run both movie and video clips on your PC.

Software called plug-ins can be downloaded onto your computer to make your Web browsing more exciting.

Lastly, the Internet started as a way of sharing information and now there are hundreds of millions of files that contain useful information covering just about every subject you can

The Microsoft Web site (http://www.microsoft.com) is the place to go if you want patches (small pieces of code to correct glitches in programs) and updates for the Windows operating system.

imagine. Information ranging from the telephone number of a local plumber to the population statistics of a country can be viewed and downloaded or printed.

● Download drawbacks

The main drawback in downloading information is that the bigger the file, the longer it takes to download. For example, a full trial version of a Microsoft product, such as Internet Explorer, is stored in a file that is between 6-17MB in size. This means that even with a high-speed modem, it would take at least a couple of

hours to transfer to your PC. In some countries, local phone calls are free, but where local calls are charged, the cost of the software is inflated by the phone charges.

● Taking time

There are many factors that affect the time it takes to transfer a file to your computer. If there are a lot of other users also trying to download the same file as you, then this will cause delays. If the file is stored on a slow computer, it will slow down the process. And if the file is stored on a computer in another country, then you are relying on the speed of the links between your Internet service provider and the other country.

You will find that, on average, a 1MB file will take around 5–10 minutes to download if you have a 56K modem (10–20 minutes if you have an older modem). Sometimes, however, you will pick a file stored on a high-speed computer at a quiet moment on the Internet and it will download quite quickly.

● Watch out for viruses

Many users worry that they might introduce a virus to their PC. Most popular Web sites are regularly scanned for viruses and software that you download is also scanned. But there is a chance of picking up a virus if you download files, so it's a good idea to install a virus detector on your PC, which you can download from the Internet (see pages 144–145).

SITES TO @ VISIT

Some Web sites are dedicated to providing a store of files that you can download to your computer at home.

This site has a powerful search facility to help you find the software you are looking for: www.shareware.com

With categories such as Education, Games, Kids and Home & Personal, this site is a vast resource of downloadable software: www.download.com

Finding a virus detector to download

You may have heard about computer viruses – programs that can wreak havoc on your computer. Virus detectors can protect your PC from infection and they're easy to download from the Internet.

IF YOU LOVE the idea of being able to download free software from the Internet, you might be reluctant to go ahead because of worries over a virus attack. A virus can, very occasionally, be transferred to your computer if you download software from the Internet and it could then damage files on your hard disk. The good news is that the threat is slight and there are special programs that can spot a virus and delete it before it does any damage.

Installing a virus detector program on your computer is a good idea and, as this type of program can be downloaded from the Internet, it provides the perfect opportunity to show the various steps involved in downloading software. Once you have downloaded the virus detector and installed the software, you can be safe in the knowledge that your computer will be protected against most future virus threats. The software will check every file on your hard disk, and any floppy disks or CD-ROMs, to make sure that there are no viruses present.

● Virus checker

There are several trial versions of virus checkers available for download from the Internet. We've chosen F-Prot Antivirus from Frisk Software International, as it's small enough to download over a normal modem (see PC Tips opposite).

Once you have downloaded and installed the software, it can be used for 30 days before it stops working. Thirty days is plenty of time to use the software to see if you like it. If you do like it and want to continue using it, you will need to buy the full program.

In order to download the virus detector (and any other file type) you first need to be connected to the Internet and have started your Web browser. Then visit the Frisk Software International Website at www.f-prot.com and follow the links to the trial software page (as shown below and opposite) in the address panel below the browser toolbar.

1 Once you have typed www.f-prot.com into your Web browser's Address box and pressed [Enter], the Frisk Software International home page loads. Click the English link.

2 The next page lists the versions of the F-Prot Antivirus programs, and there are even versions for old PCs running DOS and Linux computers. Click on the Windows link.

3 The next page lists and explains the features of this antivirus software. Scroll down the page to find the link to the trial version. Click on the download link, and on the Download center page, look for the Windows section. Click on the link for the downloadable trial version.

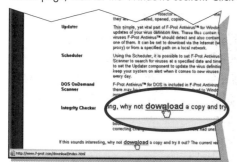

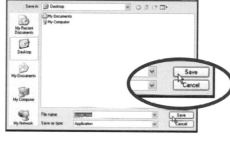

4 This Web site offers a choice of download locations. It's usually best to choose the one that's closest – in this case the European site. Click on the EXE file link to start the download process.

5 As soon as the download starts, Windows asks you what you want to do with the file you are about to download. Click the Save button in the File Download dialog box.

6 You must now choose a location for the file. Choose the Desktop by clicking on the Desktop button in the panel on the left of the Save As dialog box. This makes it very easy to locate the file later. Then click the Save button.

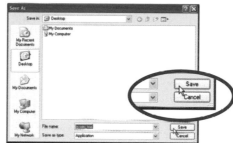

7 A new window appears and provides you with a progress summary for the download. At around 7MB, this is quite a lengthy download (see PC Tips box, below). It's best to sit back and just keep an eye on the progress bar from time to time.

8 Once the Download has completed, the progress window disappears and the icon for the file appears on the Desktop. Disconnect from the Internet and then double-click on this icon.

9 The antivirus program is now ready to install itself on your PC. Click on the Setup button to start. When the InstallShield Wizard window appears, click on the Next button.

10 Work through the on-screen instructions to install the software. Many programs offer several types of setup – it's best to choose the Typical option, if it's available.

11 When the Setup program has finished, you'll find the new program in the All Programs sub-menu on the Start menu. In this case, just select the OnDemand Scanner to start the virus checker.

AFTER 30 DAYS

If, after 30 days, you decide that you do not want to keep the F-Prot Antivirus software, you can remove it from your computer. To do this, click on the Start button, then click on the All Programs button. Select the F-Prot Antivirus folder and then click on the Uninstall entry in the sub-menu that appears. The software will be safely removed from your computer.

PC TIPS

You can download other popular anti-virus programs, including Norton Antivirus from Symantec (www.symantec.com) and VirusScan from McAfee (www.mcafee.com). However, at over 27MB and 35MB respectively, the downloadable trial versions of both programs will take a long time to download. If you can't see any information regarding file size before you start to download, check the figures in the progress window (see Step 7). You can click the Cancel button if you decide not to proceed.

Parental control programs

For concerned parents who are keen to monitor their children's use of the Internet, filter programs that screen access to certain sites and subjects are a useful aid.

Freedom – one of the Internet's most important assets – is also one of its biggest problems. Adults are at liberty to take advantage of the Net's policy on free speech and all that this entails for the content of Web sites, newsgroups and chat rooms. As a result, the Internet offers easy access to plenty of material that is inappropriate for children.

It is highly inadvisable for any child to use the Internet unsupervised because of the danger that they will (intentionally or not) come across something unpleasant. There's no easy way around this problem: the best solution is, as always, to monitor your child's surfing habits personally. But, realizing just how difficult this can be, several companies have come up with filter programs to block access to sites where unsuitable material might be found.

● Filter programs
These filters are small programs that are run automatically whenever you access the Internet. Although they vary in scope, most of the filters can

work with Web sites, but also with chat and IRC (Internet Relay Chat) channels, ftp (file transfer protocol) sites, newsgroups and email.

What the filters do is simple. As soon as you log on, they access a CAN'T GO list of 'banned' sites (or other areas of the Internet). They then check the address of any site that is requested against this list.

If the site is there, the user is blocked from entering and the site does not load. Similarly, access is denied if any site contains telltale words or phrases that appear on a master list of offending words.

Usually, each person who uses the family PC is given their own password. This allows the parents to set various levels of access for their children. Only the adult in charge has the authority to change password and access privileges. Using an Internet filter might not be perfect but it is currently the safest way to allow your children to access the Internet when using the computer unsupervised.

● What gets banned?
One problem with censorship is that the banned lists are all drawn up by groups of Americans you've never

Some Internet sites contain material unsuitable for certain surfers, but there are programs that can make these sites, or their content, unavailable.

Please enter your password to gain access to this program

FOREIGN LANGUAGE SITES

Since the Web operates globally, you might find yourself asking just how these Internet filter programs can cope with the problems of foreign languages. Not very well, is the answer, although (as usual) the programs err on the side of caution to cope with the problem. Most of the big filter programs do block areas with banned foreign words or phrases. But often these are not checked as thoroughly as English language sites, so many perfectly acceptable sites can find themselves banned as well.

met, and whose particular areas of concern you may or may not share. Concerns have been raised that many of the filters have a hidden political or religious agenda, although all the monitoring organizations deny this. Still, it has to be said that the tone adopted by some programs does seem to imply a certain moral superiority, particularly if they do not allow you to unblock sites of your choice.

To counter these worries, some of the filter makers have set up country-specific sites with their own, slightly altered lists, so you can ensure that the censor is of your own nationality and language.

● Updating the filters

There are three ways in which filters work and are maintained. The first is the way that most draft lists of restricted sites are compiled and it is also the least accurate. The filtering company simply uses special Internet search engines to find sites featuring words or phrases which are deemed restricted, or suggest that restricted content exists on that page. In some cases the area will actually be checked manually but sites are often banned automatically until someone tells the list-makers otherwise.

The second avenue is through the creators of unsuitable sites sending notification of their areas' content to the filtering companies (see Self-censorship box, below).

SELF-CENSORSHIP

Not all of the hedonistic sites that are banned by some filter programs are entirely unprincipled. The more responsible sites are well aware that their content is not suitable for children and register themselves with filter lists. By doing so, the sites not only gain a degree of moral high ground, they also make it much harder for people to complain about, or sue, them.

The third system is to set up lists of areas known to be suitable for kids. These so-called CAN GO (as opposed to CAN'T GO) lists are becoming more reliable and more popular – not only with parents seeking to guide their children but also with adult Web surfers wanting to avoid Web sites that are not of interest to them.

The problem with controlling Web access is that it's hard to tell, just by using a search engine, whether a site is merely discussing a delicate subject or actively promoting it. All filters

block obvious categories such as sexual issues, illegal activities, drugs, bigotry, racism and pornography. However, a Web site that is dedicated to fighting racism or instructing about sexually transmitted diseases often may also end up getting automatically banned until someone updates the lists by hand.

Some, but not all, filter programs allow parents to update the lists themselves. This is perhaps the only really effective way to control what's going on, allowing you to ban sites that you think are offensive and to unblock those that are no problem.

● Monitoring messages

The topics discussed by newsgroups, chat rooms and the like pose another sort of problem. In an open forum, people are free to say anything they like. This can be a major drawback to letting your children participate.

Filter programs deal with such problems in a different way: they are equipped to spot the use of a banned word or phrase instantly. They will then protect the child in a way indicated by the parent – usually by breaking the connection. However, except for special areas designed for children, newsgroups and chat rooms are no place for innocent browsers.

Internet ratings

If you use your browser for filtering which Web sites can be accessed (see page 148), how does it know which sites to allow?

There are two main systems for rating the content of Web sites – SafeSurf and the RSACi. Both are American in origin. The most popular Web browsers can make use of both systems. SafeSurf (www.safesurf.com) has been monitoring Web sites since 1995, and encouraging them to register with it. Its software, which blocks search requests using banned words or phrases, is used by many Internet Service Providers (ISPs) and also by a number of family-friendly search engines.

The acronym RSACi stands for Recreational Software Advisory Council, now managed by ICRA (the Internet Content Rating Association). Established in 1999, its goal is to set internationally recognized self-rating standards for Web content.

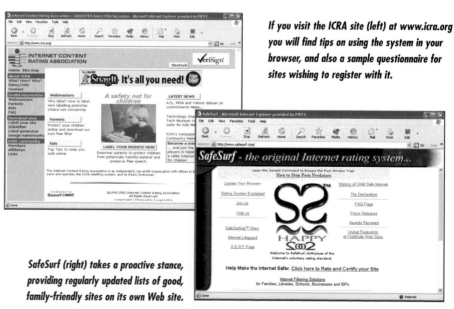

If you visit the ICRA site (left) at www.icra.org you will find tips on using the system in your browser, and also a sample questionnaire for sites wishing to register with it.

SafeSurf (right) takes a proactive stance, providing regularly updated lists of good, family-friendly sites on its own Web site.

Monitoring with Internet Explorer

Windows' Web browser, Internet Explorer, has some basic options that you can use to control access to questionable Web sites; use the Content Advisor to set it up.

1 Select Internet Explorer from the Start menu. When the Dial-up Connection dialog box appears, click the Work Offline button (you don't have to be online to change Internet Explorer's options).

2 When Internet Explorer appears, select Internet Options from the Tools menu, and then click on the Content tab. Click the Enable button in the Content Advisor box near the top of the window.

3 There are now four tabs for altering a variety of settings. The first uses the RSACi ratings (see Internet ratings, page 147) to set levels of acceptability for language, nudity, sex and violence. Just select one and move the slider to determine what is or is not allowed.

4 As you move the slider, the text underneath gives you an explanation of the types of material it will use to filter out Web sites. Set the slider for each of the four aspects listed.

5 The Approved Sites tab brings up a window allowing you to set a list of sites that are always viewable or never viewable. Just type in the URL in the top text box and then click Always or Never, as the case may be.

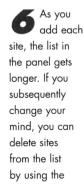

6 As you add each site, the list in the panel gets longer. If you subsequently change your mind, you can delete sites from the list by using the Remove button.

OTHER RATING SYSTEMS

Internet Explorer includes the RSACi rating system, but you can add others, such as SafeSurf (see page 147). Click on the Find Rating Systems button on the General tab and Internet Explorer takes you online to a page where you can select another system. Follow the on-screen instructions.

7 Click on the General tab, and use the first box in the User options section to indicate whether you want sites that are not covered by the rating system to be viewable. The most conservative choice is to tick this box, but you must be aware that this will block many thousands of perfectly innocent Web sites run by enthusiastic amateurs.

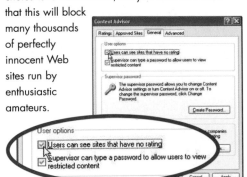

8 You should also make sure that your children cannot alter your choices. You do this by using a Supervisor Password: click the Create Password button and use the three boxes on the next dialog box to type and confirm your password and provide a hint in case you forget it.

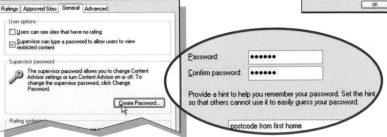

Popular filter programs

Many different filter programs are available to download; here are some of the most popular.

CYBERsitter

www.cybersitter.com

Earlier incarnations of this program came in for some criticism on the grounds of inflexibility; if a site was banned, there was no quick way you could reverse the ban.

CYBERsitter is now much more amenable to user input, and you can alter the settings in an almost infinite variety of ways. But the program has lost none of its bite: it's extremely rigorous, allowing you to block just about every possible avenue of objectionable Internet use.

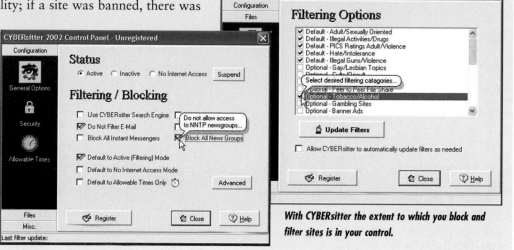

With CYBERsitter the extent to which you block and filter sites is in your control.

We-Blocker

www.we-blocker.com

Like most filtering programs, We-Blocker lets you choose which sites are and aren't accessible. By default it checks for seven categories of questionable material – pornography, violence, drugs and alcohol, gambling, hate speech, adult subjects and weaponry. You can set a different level of control for each user, which also allows you to make exceptions for specific Web sites. The We-Blocker software encourages you to keep the blocked sites database up to date, and you can block – or unblock – individual sites as you use the program. A log file record lets you keep track of your children's surfing.

We-Blocker also has word and phrase filtering which prevents children from searching for certain words. You can edit the list of prohibited words and add your own. Word filtering does slightly slow down the PC but this feature can be turned off.

Simple to use and with a filter system that works on many different levels, We-Blocker is ideal for all of the family.

MORE FILTER PROGRAMS

Cyber Patrol (www.cyberpatrol.com) and Net Nanny (www.netnanny.com) are also popular parental control programs. Both work in similar ways to the two filter programs discussed above, blocking Web sites and objectionable words.

Before buying or downloading any Web filtering programs, remember to check that they are Windows XP compatible. Visit the software company's Web site and look for the system requirements section. Windows XP is significantly different from the versions that preceded it so this type of software must be compatible with it.

Hot news on the Web

If you want to keep in touch with the latest news as it breaks or follow up a particular story in depth, why not explore the Web's fast-growing news sites?

News stories can break anywhere in the world, at any time, and conventional media can't always provide up-to-date coverage until the following day. Newspapers won't appear until the morning after and television and radio will only give so much air-time to particular stories. If you want to find out more, try the Web, where news can be kept as up-to-the-minute as television and radio – if not more so – yet it's you who chooses how much time you spend on each item.

● News online

Everybody, from the major media giants and trade organizations to enthusiastic hobbyists, is creating and maintaining Web sites that offer extensive, up-to-the-minute news on all subjects, from major international stories to purely local items.

It can be just as easy to get the latest news from the other side of the world as it is to discover more information about local issues.

Many newspapers and broadcasting companies have Web sites to provide news coverage round the clock. For example, the BBC, The Times and CNN have Web sites and there are plenty of other newspapers, television and radio stations across the globe with Web-based news services.

● Keeping in touch

Web technology means that news sites can add video and sound clips to compete with television and radio. They often have room to provide enormous amounts of background or archive data and can further extend the information with links to other relevant Web sites.

News Web sites are perfect for anyone who wants to research topical or current affairs issues, whether for homework, business or general interest. Many sites include search tools to help you find particular stories or provide help with researching online news archives.

If you're interested in specialist or local news, there's probably a Web site that can cater for you, too. You will find that subjects such as sport, entertainment, science and technology are particularly well served.

News flashes around the Web in seconds and many sites make it freely available. Today, increasingly more newspapers have associated Web sites that feature constantly updated news stories.

SITES TO @ VISIT

World news

The Web is a great way to stay in touch with news that you might not see in your local media. Here's a selection of some of the bigger national news sites:

ABC
www.abcnews.com

24-hour Italian news site
www.ilsole24ore.it

The New York Times
www.nytimes.com

Japan's Mainichi newspapers
www.mainichi.co.jp/english

Le Monde
www.lemonde.fr

Die Welt
www.welt.de

The Sydney Morning Herald
www.smh.com.au

Great news sites

There is a large – and rapidly growing – range of news sites on the Internet. Here's our guide to some of the best around.

A NEWS WEB site isn't worth its salt unless it's updated frequently enough to be topical. For general news, that means daily – and preferably more frequently, such as on the hour. However, more specialized news sites might only need to be updated once a week to give top-quality coverage. There is a huge range of fascinating sites, but not all are equally reliable. The sites featured on this page all give an excellent service.

ITN www.itn.co.uk
Independent Television News is one of the largest news providers in the world and produces TV, radio, and Multimedia news and documentaries. They provide news for ITV, Channel 4 and Channel 5 in the UK – you can find links to all these channels' Web sites on ITN's site. It also features headlines from ITV news. To find out more about any headlines, click on the text and you will be taken directly to that story on the ITV site.

BBC News http://news.bbc.co.uk
This richly informative site draws on the immense television and radio reporting resources of the BBC. The front page's headlines are updated frequently and there are in-depth sections, including sport, science/technology and business. Each story comes with a set of links to other Web sites and many stories include sound and video clips from BBC television and radio reports.

Sky Television www.sky.com/news
The strength of this satellite television's news coverage is in sports, especially football, rugby union, rugby league, golf and tennis stories. It features short, snappy reports which are updated every day and, not surprisingly, there is in-depth coverage of events where Sky has exclusive live broadcast rights, such as the Ryder Cup golf tournament.

The Independent www.independent.co.uk
The news pages of *The Independent* are updated every day and include sections for UK news, international news, business and sport. There are also areas featuring the paper's columnists, leader articles and letters from readers. If you want to have your say on topical issues, you can click on the Argument link to join in *The Independent*'s own forums.

CNN Interactive www.cnn.com
America's global television news service offers an extensive Web site, including sections for US news, world news, science/technology, sport and weather. But there is some light relief with sections about travel, and entertainment. Ecology and health are also covered.

The Guardian

www.guardianunlimited.co.uk

This umbrella site gives you access to both *The Guardian* and *The Observer* newspapers, including their weekly supplements and their Web-only offshoots. Of particular interest if you want to keep up with Web developments, is *The Guardian*'s Weblog section. If you're more interested in sport, then there are daily updated pages for football and cricket. You can also subscribe to daily electronic newsletters to get the latest news delivered to your PC every afternoon. In addition, there are comprehensive archive and search facilities.

USA Today

www.usatoday.com

The *USA Today* site is the ideal way to catch up with the national headlines in the United States. There are also regular updates covering international news, plus a money section, the latest weather reports and very comprehensive US sports coverage. This is an excellent place to keep track of all the very latest American football, baseball, basketball and ice hockey results.

The Electronic Telegraph

www.telegraph.co.uk

The Daily Telegraph's Web site is one of the best produced by a UK newspaper. Its home page gives you links to the day's lead stories. There are special sections for UK and international news, as well as weather, sport and jobs. You can see today's Matt cartoon online and even join *The Telegraph*'s crossword society to try and solve a wide range of puzzles.

The Times

www.the-times.co.uk

This Web site gives you access to online versions of *The Times*, *The Sunday Times* and two weekly publications comprising *The Times Education Supplement* and *The Times Higher Education Supplement*. It has its own Resources area, too, which lets you search through their archives of online news articles from the start of 1996 to present day.

CNet

www.cnet.com

This US-based Web-only magazine is one of the best places to get the latest computing news. There's extensive coverage of PC, Apple Macintosh and Internet technology – with reports that are updated every day. It's also worth checking out the reviews of software and hardware, and the terrific tips and tutorials. Watch out for all sorts of useful downloads in CNet's Download section.

Dotmusic

www.dotmusic.com

Dotmusic is a part of the large and successful BT Openworld network. If you want to find out about the latest chart news, get information about new releases before your friends and keep up with the dance music scene, then this is the place for you. There are music industry stories, the latest gossip and lots of sound and video downloads.

New Scientist

www.newscientist.co.uk

The New Scientist site provides authoritative science and technology news coverage. It features some of the best articles from the magazine, covering current topics from genetically modified crops to the safety of mobile phones, in a clear and accessible style. You'll also find Web-only material, archives and supplements to the magazine articles.

Sports.Com

www.sports.com

This dedicated sports news Web site concentrates on football and rugby, with player profiles, team news and all the statistics and fixture details you could hope to find. There are also sections for European leagues. Information for the sports gambler is a key element of the site, and there are links enabling you to bet online.

The Hollywood Reporter

www.hollywoodreporter.com

This is the Web version of the famous LA-based film and entertainment magazine. Every day sees newly updated film, television and music stories. The site also includes an archive section and, if you're a member, you can use this terrific area to find out the latest status of films and television programmes currently in production.

PC TIPS

How to find local news

In many places, local and regional newspapers have their own Web sites. Some local radio stations also maintain Web sites but these rarely carry much news. For this reason it's best to concentrate on finding out if your local paper is on the Net. The best tactic is to use an Internet search engine, preferably a regionally based one. If you know the name of your local newspaper, make a search using that name. If you don't, you could look in news sections using the name of your town or locality to instigate the search. Use your browser software to get to the Yahoo! UK home page at www.yahoo.co.uk. Here you'll notice a number of predefined sections – click on the Newspapers link in the News and Media section. Simply scroll down the screen and you'll find a comprehensive list of links to UK regional and national papers, from the *Barnsley Chronicle* to the *Yorkshire Post*.

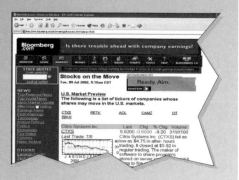

FINANCIAL NEWS

The finance industry is in the process of being revolutionized by the Internet, as companies bypass the middlemen and go straight to the wired consumers. In turn, the customers are able to use the rich information sources that the Internet can supply.

However, savings and investments are inherently complex matters, so it helps if you can get your news – and advice – in a clear and comprehensible form. The Motley Fool UK (www.fool.co.uk) is the British offshoot of its US parent. Its motto is 'educate, amuse, enrich',

and it provides financial news and background information in a clear, amusing manner. There's frequently updated news from the money markets and plenty of informed background comment.

If your investment interests range globally, then www.bloomberg. com is worth a look. This is the free Internet outpost of the professional investor's electronic news feed. As such, it is full of information on all aspects of global markets, with enough charts and graphs to keep you happy for hours.

And, if the hot new technology sector excites you, then you could do much worse than check out the Red Herring Online site (www.redherring.com), the Web version of a US magazine that is dedicated to technology news, research and analysis. This site has a snappy design with authoritative and quickly digestible content.

Sport on the Web

The Internet is a fabulous resource for sports fans. Wherever you are in the world, you can keep up with your favourite team, exchange gossip and make sure you know your idol's latest score.

It's easy to take advantage of the wealth of sports information on the Internet. You can keep up to date with a Sumo wrestling competition in Japan as easily as discovering the score of a local football match.

If you are a sports fan, you will find the Internet an amazing treasure trove of news, results and gossip. It doesn't matter what your sport is – soccer or squash, bass fishing or boules, table tennis or ten-pin bowling – there is likely to be a site out there for you. Such sites are run by both official and unofficial organizations, and most are kept constantly up to date with the latest information.

For many sports, there is a huge range of different sites to choose from. There might well be a specific area devoted to your favourite league, your local club, or even your favourite individual player.

● By the fans, for the fans
The low cost of putting information on the Internet means that a huge number of sports sites are created and run by enthusiastic amateurs.

There's always a tennis tournament on somewhere in the world, and you can follow events as they happen.

This works well, because anyone who believes they have something interesting to tell the world about their love and knowledge of, say, speed skating is limited only by the time they have to devote to it.

● Instant results
News and results are the core of any good sports site on the Web, closely followed by chat and opinion. The speed of computers means that the slicker sites will have results, match reports – and often even pictures – only minutes after the events or games finish. This is long before you read about them in the newspaper or see them on the television news.

Great sports sites

To help you get the most out of sporting information available on the Internet, here's a run-down of some of the best sports sites.

SPORTS NEWS needs to be, above all, up to date, accurate and well-informed. All of the sites selected fit the bill in all these respects.

There is a range of commercial and official sites here, from the Football Association site to the world's rugby union news, plus a selection of unofficial sites to give you a flavour of what's on offer. All the sites quoted are worth a visit if you're a general sports fan, but you will find many others if you browse the Internet, following up links.

You can rely on large publishers and official organizations for professional design and accuracy, but they are only likely to present the official line.

Club sites will also present an image that is beneficial to the club and might attempt to sell you memorabilia imprinted with the club logo as well as entrance tickets, season tickets and supporters' club membership.

For interesting, off-beat opinions and hot gossip, you might find the unofficial sites, run by enthusiasts, much more rewarding, although they cannot necessarily be relied on for either accuracy or slick design.

Sporting Life

www.sporting-life.com
This is the online version of the now defunct horse-racing enthusiast's daily newspaper. It is an excellent general sports site, covering a huge range of sports and is updated throughout the day. There's lots of hard news and a full results service.

The Sporting Life site has the latest news and results from a wide range of sports – including horse racing!

Football on the World Wide Web

There are countless football sites on the Internet. Here's a taster to kick off your footie browsing.

Chelsea Football Club

www.chelseafc.co.uk
This is the official site of Chelsea Football Club. As you would expect, it is smart and slick. There is news and feedback, fixtures lists and league tables, online shopping from the club shop and even a betting link. Like many big club sites, this is an excellent site.

Football 365

www.football365.co.uk
If you want a UK-wide view of soccer, try this site, which is part of the 365 network of Web sites. In addition to the serious news stories covering all the top clubs, the site takes a look at the lighter side of football, displaying look-alikes and recording the gaffes that soccer stars and pundits would rather forget about. Football 365 also offers plenty of ways of keeping up with what's going on if you don't want to visit every day: you can sign up for free email newsletters by typing in your email address.

Australian Coarse Angling

www.coarsefishing.ws
There are plenty of fishing sites on the Internet, and this one is particularly well designed and clearly laid out. The site is informative, attractive, comprehensive and humorous, with sections that cover everything from bait to floats and rods.

GolfWeb

www.golfweb.com
This US site is a huge compendium of everything you could want to know about the world of golf. There is opinion, latest tournament news, listings of future events and participating players, and fun stuff, such as fantasy golf.

Tennis Magazine Online

www.tennis.com
The Internet outpost of the US magazine *Tennis* has loads of news and feature material, as well as detailed archive sections on the year's Grand Slam events.

Tennis is well represented on the Net. Other popular sports with plenty of sites include golf and cricket. Most sports sites offer a huge range of information which is much more up to date than you could expect from a conventional magazine.

Cricket

www.uk.cricket.org
You'll find just about everything of interest in the world of cricket on this site. There are current test match scores and reports, player information, a breakdown of news from the main cricket-playing countries, a forum where fans can discuss matches and even live coverage of far-flung test cricket.

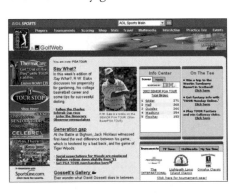

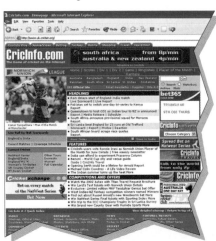

THE 2004 OLYMPIC GAMES

The Olympics is the mega-event of the sporting calendar. The 2004 games are to be held in Athens, which is the birthplace of the Olympics. The official site (www.athens.olympics.org) tells you plenty about the competitions, and has lots of information on the culture and ceremonies that are a large part of the event. There is also a calendar of events and a brief history of the original Olympics. For further information on the 2004 Olympics, and regular updates, it is worth looking at the Web site of the Greek embassy's Press office (www.greekembassy.org/press/2004updates).

Scrum.com

www.scrum.com

This round-up of the world's rugby union news is updated daily. There is masses of comment from every conceivable angle on all the current talking points, listings of all fixtures and results, as well as reports on past matches.

NZRugby.com

www.nzrugby.com

The awesome All Blacks have a suitably impressive Web presence, cleverly designed and packed with information on everything you want to know, including the famous Haka.

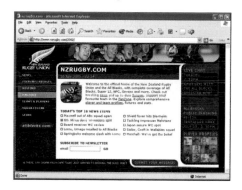

Ski central

www.skicentral.com

This site is one of the best for skiing and snowboarding aficionados, and has plenty of links to related winter sports sites.

Sportquest

www.sportquest.com

SIRC is a sports research organization distributing information on virtually any sport you can think of to coaches, sportsmen and women and fitness institutes. The site has an exhaustive list of sport-related links.

SumoWeb!

www.sumoweb.com

Sumo wrestling has a large presence on the Internet. Start by getting to grips with this excellent site.

The Football Association

www.thefa.com

There's always space for more footie sites and the official site of the Football Association is attractive, informative and comprehensive.

FIFA

www.fifa.com

This excellent site is the official Internet home of FIFA, the governing body of world football. It's got everything from world rankings to updates on changes to the rules. It also features fascinating news and views for football fans worldwide.

SITES TO @ VISIT

Even if you're not a major fan of any one sport, there may be links that will help you discover a new hobby.

Boomerangs

www.flight-toys.com/boomerangs.htm

A special-interest site, this has an exhaustive choice of links to sites dealing with boomerangs.

Yachting

www.yachtsandyachting.com

This contains all the latest yachting news and race results, as well as information on weather conditions and events.

● **Acknowledgments**
Abbreviations: t = top; b = bottom; r = right;
l = left; c = centre; bkg = background.
All cartoons are by Chris Bramley

  8   Steve Bartholomew/De Agostini
 10   Steve Bartholomew/De Agostini
 14   De Agostini
 15   Steve Bartholomew/De Agostini
 18   Tony Stone Images
 22   The Stockmarket
 26   Steve Bartholomew/De Agostini
 26   Lyndon Parker/De Agostini
 30   (computer) De Agostini (Shakespeare)
      Getty One Stone
 32   Steve Bartholomew/De Agostini
 33   Steve Bartholomew/De Agostini
 34   Steve Bartholomew/De Agostini
 36   Getty One Stone
 40t Steve Bartholomew/De Agostini
 40b Steve Bartholomew/De Agostini
 41bl Steve Bartholomew/De Agostini
 41br Steve Bartholomew/De Agostini
 44   Steve Bartholomew/De Agostini
 46   De Agostini
 50   De Agostini
 54   Steve Bartholomew/De Agostini
 56   Steve Bartholomew/De Agostini
 58   Lyndon Parker
 60   Lyndon Parker, (planets) NASA
 61tl NASA
 62   Lyndon Parker/De Agostini

 64   Barratt East London
 66   Images Colour Library
 68   De Agostini
 72   De Agostini
 76   De Agostini
 78   Lyndon Parker
 82   Lyndon Parker
 84   De Agostini
 88   De Agostini
 92   t Steve Bartholomew/De Agostini; c
      Courtesy Labtec; b Courtesy Sony
 93   Steve Bartholomew/De Agostini
 94   t Steve Bartholomew/De Agostini; b
      De Agostini
 95b Steve Bartholomew/De Agostini
 96t Steve Bartholomew/De Agostini
 97all Steve Bartholomew/De Agostini
 98   Lyndon Parker
 99all Lyndon Parker
100   t Images Colour Library; b Lyndon
      Parker
104all Steve Bartholomew/De Agostini
105   b WACOM Europe GmbH; 105 t, c
      Steve Bartholomew/De Agostini
106   tr Palm Europe Ltd; l, c, r, bl, bc Steve
      Bartholomew/De Agostini
107all Warrender Grant
108   t Lyndon Parker; c Microsoft
      Corporation
110   Steve Bartholomew/De Agostini
111   tr Creative Labs (UK) Ltd; br Sony
      Computer Entertainment Europe;

      tr Kingston Technology Europe Limited;
      cl, cr Plus Group PR
114tr Getty One Stone
115tr Getty One Stone
116cl Getty One Stone
118   tr NASA; b NASA
119tl NASA
122   Quadrant Picture Library
123   Image Bank
124   Steve Bartholomew/De Agostini
126all Steve Bartholomew/De Agostini
127cl Kobal Collection/©Disney
      Enterprises, Inc
128tr Kobal Collection (courtesy MGM)
128all De Agostini
136   Steve Bartholomew/De Agostini
138   De Agostini
142l Steve Bartholomew/De Agostini
142r Getty One Stone
143   Image Bank
144   (computer) Steve Bartholomew/
      De Agostini; (syringe) Telegraph
      Colour Library
146   Lyndon Parker/De Agostini
150   (computer) Lyndon Parker; (globe)
      Stockmarket
153r Hulton Getty
154   (sports people) Allsports; (globe &
      web) The Image Bank
155c De Agostini
156   tr, bl De Agostini
157   br De Agostini